ECHOES

Tales and Legends of
Bedfordshire and Hertfordshire

Vic Lea

with line drawings by
Ray Aspden

The
Book
Castle

First published November 1988
by
The Book Castle
12 Church Street
Dunstable
Bedfordshire, LU5 4RU

Reprinted 1989, 1991

© Vic Lea (text) 1988
© Ray Aspden (drawings) 1988

ISBN 0 9509773 9 X

Printed and bound by:
Antony Rowe Ltd., Chippenham

Contents

ECHOES

A horrific train crash in which three goods trains collide in the
long WELWYN tunnel. Two small children had been smuggled
aboard one of the freight trains and become tragic victims. Their
identity is unknown to this day.
(Originally featured in Hertfordshire Countryside)

A celebrated ELSTREE murder of a card sharp whose body is
hidden in a garden fish-pond. A wife forces her man to give
king's evidence to save his neck.
(Originally heard on BBC Radio)

A ghost story, now part of a family history. An Irish boy with a
damaged leg becomes a lodger with two elderly folk living close
to LUTON's Airport. His sudden death in a road accident is
unknown to them, but his shoes tell the story.
(Originally featured in Luton News)

The Portuguese Treasury suddenly become aware that a major
currency has been duplicated . . . and with genuine notes. The
stability of the nation is in question. Waterlows of
DUNSTABLE are blamed, but they are just one of the many
dupes in the greatest currency swindle of all time.
(Originally heard on BBC Radio)

FOREWORD

In presenting this volume, the author Vic Lea, having gathered together a unique collection of stories, has drawn on records which cover a long stretch of time.

After countless hours of painstaking research, the following journal will provide the reader with a clear and detailed account of events and circumstances which touched the lives of ordinary people. Despite many radical changes throughout the years our nation has retained numerous characteristics of life in earlier times.

Although the main purpose of this writing is intended to be informative, I can assure the unwary purchaser who has the good fortune to read this book that he will find the contents equally entertaining.

F. Norris.

Under the foot
   beyond the eye,
Here are the tales
   of a time gone by,
When horses hoofs
   made common clatter
And crimes did fashion
   local chatter.

Tommy Rose.

Author's Acknowledgements

The passage of time leaves but scant evidence
of the struggles of man.
Few are the records of common folk and the many
events which fashioned the topics
of yester-year.

Much is to be said, then, for present-day newspaper
and magazine editors that they saw fit to enlighten their
readers and to remind them of their heritage with
these deeds and misdeeds of our ancestors.
Many are the lessons that such tales may hold for both
present and future generations.

My most cordial thanks are due to the following, under whose
banner some of these tales first appeared and who have
kindly consented for them to be reprinted here:

HERTFORDSHIRE COUNTRYSIDE

THE LUTON NEWS

THE DUNSTABLE GAZETTE

BEDFORDSHIRE MAGAZINE

BEDFORDSHIRE and NORTHAMPTONSHIRE LIFE

and

THE BRITISH BROADCASTING CORPORATION,
RADIO BEDFORDSHIRE

Night Ride

It was two small mounds in the Welwyn church-yard that excited Branch Johnson. Hertfordshire's celebrated historian had discovered the graves of two unnamed children and hoped to solve an age-old mystery. And as a renowned Welwyn worthy, he had been most interested in the records of an inquest held on the 12th of June 1866 at the Cowper Arms in Welwyn. But probe as he might, Branch Johnson found that he could add little to that reported some one hundred odd years earlier.

For it was known then that some unknown person had smuggled two small children into the Midland Railway's goods yard in London under cover of night. They were placed in an empty wagon, one of a long line awaiting despatch, and prepared for an arduous journey to the north. The freight waggons of those days were high-sided affairs and made of wood throughout. And this caused the historian to believe that their transport was a matter of urgency, and probably tempered by desperation. For the cost of passenger travel in those days was known to be excessive. But the Midland freight was bound for Bedford, and since the St. Pancras extension had yet to be completed, it was using Great Northern rails and diverting at Hitchin on to the now dis-used Midland branch through Shefford. Accordingly the historian deduced that the children's destination was Bedford and that someone conversant with freight movement at that place, intended to meet them. For they could not have scaled the sides themselves. The report showed the girl was about seven years of age and the boy barely five years old. They were well dressed and seemed to have been carefully nourished. But who they were, and whence they came, was as much speculation as their intended destination. But their death was no mystery. For these unfortunate children were the victims of the most horrendous accident in rail history.

It was approaching 10 pm on the Saturday evening of June the ninth 1866, when a Great Northern freight train began its journey to the north. It had a clear run through Hertfordshire, for then as now, freight trains almost dominated the metals at night. But as it passed the Welwyn signal box and rattled through the short northern tunnel, the engine seemed to lose power. And when the train entered the second and longer tunnel it ground to a halt. A steam pipe had fractured. Fireman Andrew Gray climbed down and walked back into the tunnel to warn the guard and his companion that one of them would need to go back to the Welwyn box and request a relief engine. There was no fear of imminent disaster as they were sure that signalman James Bradfield in the Welwyn box would halt any following train until he received the Line 'All Clear' sign from the more northern Knebworth signal box. But one of those signalmen made a mistake, and the subsequent enquiry failed to establish guilt. For the Bedford bound, Midland train was following and was given clearance to proceed, with the result that it piled into the stationary Great Northern train, killing the guard and mortally injuring his relief man, John Rawlings. The collision had caused a derailment, and damaged waggons blocked the twin-track tunnel. But hardly had this happened when a fast London-bound freight entered the tunnel from the north. The crash was devastating. The engine and tender and five of the waggons left the rails and rolled on their sides. The furnace doors burst open and flaming coals cascaded on to the wrecked waggons. A fire broke out and spread so rapidly that the tunnel became a blazing inferno within seconds. Amazingly all three engine crews had escaped serious injury and they hastened to raise the alarm. A message was telegraphed to the line engineer at Hatfield who with a force of volunteers raced to the scene. Hampered by a scarcity of water and fire-fighting equipment, their efforts to drag out burning waggons were thwarted by suffocating smoke and intense heat. But help arrived in the shape of an area superintendent, two hundred men and a huge steam crane. The combined force managed to extract sixteen burning waggons of the one hundred and eight involved. And one of those pulled clear contained the bodies of the two children. They had been suffocated. But the fire raged on, and it was finally decided in the early hours of the Sunday morning to let it burn itself out. With the whole line from London to Peterborough closed down, national attention centred on the outcome. But it was six pm on the Sunday evening before a thorough investigation was possible.

The debris was cleared and the tunnel inspected for structural damage. But it was found that the sides and roofing were composed of five rings of brick and had weathered the fire. The damage was

superficial, and therefore the safety of the structure had not been impaired. But news reporters had flocked to the scene. Even papers in far off Glasgow featured the item, while the London Illustrated News carried a graphic picture of the carnage. So it was that the little Welwyn Cowper Arms was crowded as the inquest took place.

Signalman Bradfield swore that he had received an 'All Clear' signal from the Knebworth box that night, and Harding in that box was adamant that he had not. So it was that blame was not attributed to either and the railway company accepted liability. They were responsible for their employees, the dead guard and his companion, but they held no brief for the children, who, as far as they were concerned, were stow-aways, and had no right of passage. Some three days later they were buried at parish expense, for no one knew who they were, and so they remain the unknown mites of the great Welwyn Tunnel crash.

One Dupe too Many

It was just an ordinary, garden fish-pond, a common place addition to grounds today as in the nineteenth century, but this one figured prominently in a murder case that captured the interest of the nation. And it was on the evidence of its owner, Mrs Sarah Probert, that the criminals were brought to book. For she had been looking out of her bedroom window late one summer night, when she saw three shadowy figures cross her lawn. Something in her ornamental pond seemed to interest them. But when they resorted to the use of a horse to drag out a bulky object, she was most alarmed and had good reason so to be, for one figure she recognised as that of her own husband.

It had all begun with John Thirkell's visit. He had befriended her husband, William, in the spring of 1822. He was a rich man, she knew. His father was the Mayor of Norwich and the head of a clothing empire. But Sarah Probert did not know that son John had proved a disappointment and had refused to follow in his father's footsteps, or that the worthy mayor had purchased commissions in the army and then the navy for his erring son. But John Thirkell had been thrown out of both services and had resorted to a life of loose living, long before he was twenty five.

But the packed court at Hertford heard more about John Thirkell. He had opened a clothing store in the fashionable part of London, and after a mere three months of trading the whole place was destroyed by fire. The insurance company suspected arson and took Thirkell to court on the issue. But they lost their case and had to pay John Thirkell an enormous sum. His next enterprise saw Thirkell purchase the Cock Tavern in the Haymarket, and from the outset he did everything he could to encourage the patronage of London's well-britched sporting fraternity. The venture flourished. But one of his customers turned out to be a dapper, little fellow, named William Weare, who seemed to know everyone worth knowing and was reputed to be on intimate terms with members of the nobility. John Thirkell just had to retain this man's patronage, so he showered the fellow with gifts and lavish treatment. When Weare suggested that as a means to encourage the very rich a card school would be most enticing, Thirkell fell for it. And as it was most appropriate that the mine host be present in the early games, he also tried his hand. But he soon discovered that things were very wrong . . . the games were rigged. Mr. Weare and the men he had introduced to the game were members of a card-sharp organisation and he, John Thirkell, was the Dupe and he had lost a lot of money. But the mine host was too astute to reveal his feelings and made an excuse not to play further games while he thought of a way to wreak revenge upon the man who had fooled him so easily. That opportunity soon presented itself. For John Thirkell had enjoyed several weekends at Probert's country cottage near Elstree, and when that worthy invited him for a shoot and a few days in rural Elstree, Thirkell promptly asked Weare to accompany him, and the unsuspecting card-sharp readily accepted.

The stage was set. John Thirkell met Weare on the Tyburn turnpike, close to present day Marble Arch, and together they travelled in Thirkell's gig into Hertfordshire.

According to the evidence at the subsequent trial, Thirkell had already arranged for Weare's murder. He had enlisted the aid of a notorious criminal commonly known as George Hunt, and with Probert they were to meet Thirkell in the lanes about Elstree and there kill the card-sharp and rob him. But things went wrong. Thirkell's accomplices were not at the appointed place, and what was more William Weare had become alarmed. So much so that he had jumped out of the gig and was running down the lane towards the village. Thirkell had to act alone, and pulling out a pistol hidden under his seat, he shot the fleeing man in the shoulder and slew him with a knife. But so intent was he on robbing the body and then dragging it out of sight into the hedgerows that he overlooked his knife and pistol and left hurriedly without them. He met Probert and Hunt at the cottage, and having shared out the loot behaved as though nothing had happened. Thirkell even gave the unsuspecting Mrs Probert a gift of the dead man's gold watch and chain, claiming it as his own. It was then that Thirkell had doubts about his lost weapons and the hidden body. So the three men went to the spot after dark and hoisted Weare's corpse on to a small cart, but search as they might the weapons were not to be found. But their activities set off dogs barking in a nearby farm and they heard the occupants, roused by the noise, come out to investigate. The miscreants departed in haste and reaching

Probert's cottage dumped the body in the garden fish pond. But Probert insisted they move it to the deeper and remote field pond in the adjoining meadow and during the following night they accomplished the move.

Next day Thirkell and George Hunt returned to London but in Elstree rumours were circulating. Folk had heard Weare screaming and two labourers had discovered a pistol and a blood-stained knife. Sarah Probert was most concerned and confronted her husband with his strange behaviour concerning her fish-pond. And at last he confessed and related all he knew. But Sarah Probert did all she could to save her man. She insisted that he give himself up and by relating all he knew give king's evidence against his former colleagues. This he did, and word was soon sent to Bow Street, London, and Thirkell and Hunt were quickly taken into custody and held until the trial at Hertford where the grim story unfolded.

John Thirkell was executed on the 9th of January 1824, an occasion that attracted the largest crowd on record. It is said that over 15,000 folk crammed into Hertford to watch on that day. Hunt escaped the noose, only to be sentenced to serve in the penal colonies for the rest of his life. But of course William Probert, for giving king's evidence, was set free. However a year later he was found guilty of stealing a horse, and he ended his life on the gallows as a common thief.

Restless Shoes

On the night of 24th September 1940, German raiders dropped two parachute mines on Luton's airport. The first, however, fell short of its target severely damaging nearby cottages. But for the residents of one, it also registered a strange event. One of a series, so marked and macabre, that the saga has since become a family legend.

Almost on the fringe of Luton, close to the now internationally known airport, stands a row of small country cottages. In 1940, they were the only dwellings near to the then newly built Luton Airport. The Crick family lived in No. 1. They were sensible, reliable working-class people, and everyone who knew Ernie, who worked in the adjacent aircraft factory, and Emily, his wife, liked and respected them.

With the outbreak of war, their two sons were soon in uniform, and Emily took up a job in the factory canteen as an antidote for the anxiety and sadness she felt for her boys. A quietness possessed the house which it had never known since the Cricks had lived in it.

Ernie and Emily, however, were not destined to be lonely long. They were to have a new companion, and one who was destined to provide them, as well as countless others, with one of the most intriguing and astonishing mysteries ever.

David Bicker was the name of the stranger who knocked on their door one morning. It was Emily who opened it to a slender, over-pale and pathetic-looking youth, who could not have have been more than eighteen years old. His clothes were shabby, and his features told a story of failing health.

He explained that he had only recently left a hospital bed in Ireland where, as the result of a motor cycle accident, it had been necessary to amputate his left leg. He was fit now, and on the lookout for work and for somewhere to live.

Emily noticed that he had not yet properly mastered the movements of an artificial limb, a fact which served to further excite her compassion. As for her husband, he took to the youth at once, and he was particularly impressed with the way in which he kept his shoes. They were old and much worn, but they shone brightly – the obvious result of repeated, thorough polishing. That was seen as a sign of respectability and of moral worth. David Bicker was accepted as a lodger by Ernie and Emily Crick.

The relationship developed so quickly that soon the youth might have been their own son, and indeed, a sort of sixth sense seemed to link the boy with them. Sometimes they could even feel his presence, when he was nowhere near them, and this strange relationship resulted in mysterious incidents.

The first curious happening occurred when Ernie narrowly escaped serious injury at work. Emily was working in her kitchen when she saw David's face suddenly ashen; the boy toppled and fell heavily as he blacked out completely. When he came round, he told her that her husband was quite safe, although she had no idea that he had been in danger. Nevertheless, when Ernie came home that evening, he said that he had narrowly missed being involved in a very serious accident.

It was this curious awareness on David Bicker's part that undoubtedly saved Emily's life only a few days later.

A quiet evening followed a day of air-raid alarms, and the Cricks and their lodger had retired to bed. Mrs Crick became aware of a dog barking, and she heard David get out of his bed. Ernie, too, was restless and he called out to David. Suddenly the youth came into their room.

"Please, get up. I feel that something terrible is going to happen."

Thinking the boy was in the throes of a nightmare, Ernie got up and pushed David into his own room. At that moment a brilliant flash lit up the landscape as brightly as noon-day. David snatched the eiderdown from his bed, dashed past Ernie into Emily's room and flung the quilt about her at the very moment she was in the act of rising.

In that same instant the walls of the house rocked, the windows disintegrated in countless fragments which were spattered over the room like bullets. To a roaring sound that filled the air and threatened to burst their eardrums, the front of the cottage collapsed. A parachute mine had landed in the garden.

Sometime later, Ernie and Emily examined their bedding. It had been cut into shreds by flying glass. Emily, though badly cut about the legs, had been saved from more serious injury by David's prompt action. As for the boy himself, he was not so much as scratched!

Yet much stranger things were to come. The house was repaired,

Emily recovered, and the Crick home settled down again to its accustomed routine. It was then that David met a former school-boy friend of his, and he not only changed his job to work beside the lad but also went to live with the boy's parents in Watford. But David always returned to Luton and the Cricks every week-end, coming and going as he pleased and always receiving a welcome as though he was their own son.

Returning from a shopping expedition one day Emily found that David, who had been staying for the week-end, had gone. On the kitchen table he had left a note and some money for his keep for his two days with them. The note asked Emily to take his shoes, which he had left in the kitchen cupboard, to the cobbler's. He promised to call for them the following week-end. Emily did as requested, collecting the shoes a few days later, and giving them an extra shine with her duster before placing them in the cupboard to await their owner.

But he never came.

The weeks passed, but brought no word of David. Ernie went on to night work, and Emily, alone in the house, began to hear strange noises. At first, hearing the creakings on the stairs, Emily was frightened. But as she listened, tight-lipped, she realised that she had heard the same kind of footsteps before. They were so familiar as to be quite unmistakable. They were David's. For that was the way he had climbed the stairs when he came in late, softly and considerately, determined not to disturb those in bed. Emily was scared no more.

The weeks grew into months, and more than two years passed, but there was no word of David Bicker. Emily often looked at his shoes in the cupboard, wondering what could have happened to their owner. And she was made to wonder all the more because of the mysterious state of the shoes. They were always clean. During all the time they had lain there not a speck of dust had settled on them! On everything else in that cupboard, including her own and Ernie's shoes, a film of dust collected in a few days. David's shoes, however, remained bright and shiny.

Night after night, the footsteps sounded on the stairs, and sometimes so distinctly that Emily had to investigate. There was never anyone there, but always her thoughts turned to those shoes in the cupboard.

Then, one morning, a letter arrived, the envelope bearing an Irish post-mark. Ernie opened it, read the contents and handed it to Emily without saying a word. It was a single sheet of paper, and it was from David's mother. It seemed that she had mislaid the Cricks' address and had taken nearly three years to trace it.

"I suppose you know about David", the letter said. "I still cannot believe it is true."

David Bicker had been killed in a road accident the very morning he left the Cricks' cottage, almost three years earlier. All the time they had been ignorant of his fate, but now that they knew a strange thing happened. There was no sound of footsteps on the stairs. The old quiet had returned to the cottage.

But something more astonishing happened next, and something which remains one of the most bewildering mysteries of the century. For on the following morning when Emily opened the cupboard what she saw so amazed her that she straightaway called for her husband.

Together, they stared in bewildered silence at the shoes which for so long had remained so scrupulously clean on the shelf. David Bicker's shoes were shiny no longer.

They had turned green with mildew overnight.

The Day a Nation Trembled

There was nothing unusual about the luxurious chauffeur-driven limousine that nosed out of a Dunstable side street to join an escort of police cars enroute for London. Few knew that the dapper little man reclining in the rear seat held a specially constructed suitcase between his knees which held £500,000 in bank notes. Even those entrusted with the secret had no cause to consider that incident other than mere routine. For the scene had been enacted five times without incident before.

The officer in charge of the escort noted that the man with the suitcase seemed particularly on edge this trip. However, it seemed natural that he should with so much money in his charge. The escorting cars moved closer to the limousine, the officers preparing for immediate action should the need arise.

But it was not the prospect of highway robbery that caused Robert Margang to perspire so freely on that trip. His fear issued from the thought of discovery on this – his last trip. For, although they did not know it, those police officers were actually guarding one of the most audacious criminals of all time, and they were escorting the last consignment of his haul – £3,000,000 in all.

The first moves of this fantastic coup began with Margang and six others meeting in secret in Brussels. From that moment moves began to edge specially selected associates into important posts within the Portuguese Treasury and within the Bank of Portugal. They even got a man placed in that nation's Foreign Office.

On December 4th 1924, the smooth tongued Margang and an accomplice arrived in England and a day later they called upon Sir William Waterlow, head of the distinguished Dunstable printing firm. For some considerable time Waterlows had been printing currency notes for several continental countries, including Portugal. They were enjoying a world-wide reputation.

Margang had secured documents seemingly from an impeccable source. They gave him authority to place an order with the firm for the printing of bank notes to the value of £3,000,000. These notes were to be issued and used only in the Portuguese colony of Angola. The notes were to carry the picture of the poet Devas and a special series of numbers was raised to cover the entire issue.

So good were the documents submitted by Margang that Sir William was completely deceived, especially after the fellow requested that he should contact the Portuguese Treasury on the matter of the Devas printing plates. For Margang had made a serious mistake at this point.

Waterlows had not been connected with the previous Devas issue, and the plates were with another printing firm in Germany. But the arch-crook had acted swiftly, covering his error by suggesting that permission might be obtained to use those Portuguese plates that were still in Waterlows' possession. These carried a picture of the head of Vasco da Gama, and since the company had already completed a large order for this series they were holding the plates in bond following indications of a pending follow-up order, which in fact, was ultimately cancelled.

Sir William, on Margang's direction, then contacted an official in the Portuguese Treasury. Of course he was one of the gang, and accordingly he answered Sir William's communication, giving permission for the use of the Vasco da Gama plates, and advising that in this instance these notes upon arrival in Portugal would be over-stamped by the Treasury with the legend:

'For circulation in Angola only'

Waterlows were convinced and immediately the firm set to work to produce the issue. Margang and his accomplice were housed in the Sugar Loaf Hotel, Dunstable, and a car complete with chauffeur placed at their disposal.

When the first consignment, which amounted to the value of £380,000 was ready, Margang directed the necessary security arrangements. Eventually he saw his colleague secretly depositing Waterlows' specially ordered case, containing the money, in a luggage depository at Liverpool Street railway station in London. It was collected three days later by another of the gang who then smuggled it out of the country on board a Dutch tramp steamer.

Five consignments followed, and Margang, on the night preceeding the final trip, had the audacity to hold a farewell party, before slipping out of the country the next day without anyone in Britain being aware that a fantastic swindle had been successfully accomplished. The gang lost little time cashing in. They opened a bank in Lisbon, establishing it as the Banko Angola, and from this they bought all the foreign currency they could, using the Margang engineered issue in exchange. Thus the gang got the money into world wide circulation, and within six months they had passed off more than two million pounds, in notes that the Portuguese Government had never authorised, and what is more knew nothing about. Margang and his associates had planned well and at the first sign of danger their well-placed underlings flashed a warning.

Suddenly the Portuguese Treasury was shaken by the discovery that several foreign countries held notes that had duplicates in circulation within the country. The Treasury was most alarmed, especially when it was realised that the nation's economy was at risk. A frantic search followed and revealed that many of the transactions originated from the bank which the gang had set up, and immediately orders were given to raid the place. In the cellars of the premises three cases were found which were ultimately proved to be of those supplied by Waterlows. Some unspent money was also found, and the hunt for the swindlers begun. But the gang had scattered, and those persons questioned by the police proved to be mere employees who knew little of their masters or of their whereabouts and nothing about the actual swindle.

Some six months later Margang gave himself up to the authorities in Holland and was duly transported back to Portugal. But the ace-crook knew what he was doing, and, with the aid of some very skilful lawyers, put up a remarkable and most successful defence. He was portrayed as only a semi-innocent agent, and secured a mere eight months prison sentence. This he appears to have served with great fortitutde, after which he tactfully disappeared, no doubt to enjoy the proceeds of his carefully laid and remarkably successful plans.

*   *   *

Finally, in November 1930, the Portuguese Government brought an action in the English courts against the firm of Waterlows. There was no suggestion of the firm's dishonesty, only on the point of negligence was the suit based.

The Lord Chancellor, however, pointed out that the Bank of Portugal was a bank of issue, and could at any time secure foreign currency at the current rate with its duplicated currency. Therefore, he contended, these notes had real value. But two of the lords disagreed. They argued that these notes were not backed with gold, that the only loss sustained by the Bank of Portugal was the actual cost of printing which amounted

to £8,000, and that the notes could be replaced by the bank with a genuine issue, as indeed, they ultimately did. Therefore, these lords maintained, the sole loss to the bank was in the value of the paper.

However, after what seemed a successful defence, Waterlows were again required to sustain an appeal imposed by the Portuguese Government. This time the courts found for the bank and ordered Waterlow and Sons to pay the enormous sum of £610,395 which was met most promptly by the firm although it nearly caused their ruin. They took many, many years to recover from that set-back, but they did, retaining their dignity despite the knowledge that Margang and his fellow crooks were probably enjoying the fruits of their ill-gotten gains.

A Man to Remember

It was during the mid-summer of 1925 when a strange, elderly Frenchman came to Harpenden and searched for a grave in St. Nicholas's churchyard. For several minutes he stood over the grave as though deep in thought, and then left as mysteriously as he had come. He was Captain Alfred Dreyfus, and that fleeting visit brought many bitter memories, for the grave contained the man who had sent him to prison on the infamous Devil's Island on a false charge. Count Jean de Voilement had fled to England and spent his last days in the pleasant Hertfordshire countryside, while his countryman struggled to remove the stain of the greatest cover-up in French history.

For it was sometime in the late 1890s that the French Government became aware that someone was leaking information to the Germans. The intelligence department was alerted and eventually prepared a list of suspects for government scrutiny. But someone in office decided that the culprit must be in the army and directed attention to an officer in the French artillery regiment. So it was that Captain Alfred Dreyfus, a man of impeccable character and distinguished military record was suddenly arrested and charged with the crime. He was quickly hauled before a military court martial, and in very suspicious haste found guilty and duly sentenced to life imprisonment on the infamous prison in tropical Cayenne.

And that, as far as the Government were concerned, was the end of the matter. But they had not reckoned with the French public, for the affair had caused wide-spread alarm and several leading newspapers continued to highlight the issue. Candid questions were asked, and in their urgent desire to close the matter the French War Ministry issued a document which purported to prove Dreyfus's guilt. But it was a blunder with far reaching consequences, for the popular French

newspaper L'Eclair seized the opportunity to employ a nationally famous handwriting expert who declared that it was a forgery. The following months saw the nation divided on the issue, but when the great French literary favourite, Emile Zola, opposed the Government's handling of the matter in an out-spoken article, all France was agog. Again came a ministerial blunder. Zola was prosecuted and sentenced to twelve months imprisonment and heavily fined. But before he could be arrested, his friends contrived his escape to England, where he remained for nearly two years.

Meanwhile the Government of France was undergoing great pressure, and according to L'Eclair, men in high office were trembling. But by this time Alfred Dreyfus was little more than a fever-wracked wreck, and there was hope in some quarters that the matter would end with his demise. However, Mathieu, Dreyfus's brother, petitioned the Government to release all the papers concerning the trial. When the German Kaiser decided to show his hand and let it be known that he knew Dreyfus was innocent, it caused international concern. Panic was evident when Colonel Henry of the War Ministry tried to relieve the pressure. He adroitly altered, added to and completely changed the context of an important trial document before public release. Once again, French officialdom had misjudged the public mood, for the document was challenged on the grounds of authenticity by almost every influential body in France. So great was the outcry that Colonel Henry broke down and confessed. The following day the War Ministry issued an announcement that he had committed suicide, but L'Eclair insisted that he was only a spokesman, and that the arch-criminal, and probably the actual traitor, was still at large in Government office.

So it was that suspicion fell upon Count de Voilement, and one daring columnist implied that the fellow was directly involved. Suddenly, instead of issuing a rebuttal, as every one expected, Count de Voilement made a dash across the Channel to England and applied for sanctuary. However his schemes had embroiled others, and they continued to hold Dreyfus. But at last he was released, a fragile shadow of his former self, and although much was made of him, it actually took an Act of Parliament before he was re-instated. Meanwhile Count de Voilement had settled in Harpenden, and until his death in May 1923, took a daily stroll among the ferns and bracken of Harpenden Common.

The Wicked Lady

It was in the spring of 1660, when the news of the impending return of the exiled Charles II to these shores dominated every conversation. But there was, perhaps, one small community in which the topic did not receive so much attention, for here a strange revelation in local events had cast the national news into the shadows. That incident was so marked that generations of local folk yet unborn were to be acquainted with its curious ramifications.

A legend was born.

Today every Markyate child knows that the Wicked Lady once lived in the ancient mansion that sits serenely on the left bank of a small depression just north of the village. Most of them learn at a tender age the story of how servants of this house discovered the blood-stained body of their mistress, strangely clad in male garments. Her death, it seems, resulted from the loss of blood issuing from a bullet wound in the right shoulder.

There was a horse too, a large powerful creaure which apart from having a white flash on each foreleg was silky black throughout. That was roaming free within the grounds, and its flanks were caked with blood and lather. But none of the mansion staff could identify it as from the mansion stables. Yet there were many who readily recognised it as the mount of a mysterious miscreant, a person of great daring and of callous disposition, who had virtually terrorised the district for the past month or so.

That the reign of terror had abruptly ceased seemed conclusive evidence. Other subsequent revelations substantiated this belief.

For almost a century Markyate Cell had been the home of the wealthy, noble Ferrers family, who had taken great interest in the welfare of local people. At one time it was a large family, then from about 1635 a succession of deaths began which whittled down the household to the ageing father, Sir George, and his sole surviving son, named Sir Knighton.

At the age of thirty-five Sir Knighton married a beautiful young heiress, the Lady Kathleen Walters of Hertingford, and there were hopes that the line would survive through this union. However Sir Knighton died within a year of the marriage, just two weeks before his child was born. It was a girl.

Three months later, old Sir George died and was buried with his son at Flamstead, leaving the infant as the sole heir to one of the most coveted fortunes in the county.

The quarrel between Charles I and his Parliament was entering a critical stage when the Ferrers widow returned to her own home with her baby. There she was soon to be accosted by a rapscallion member of the Fanshawe family, whose deeds and reputation had earned him many enemies. Sir Simon Fanshawe succeeded in marrying the widow and, having secured her personal fortune, left her for a life of gaiety and loose living.

The Civil War saw the Fanshawes racing to the King's colours, Sir Simon among them. Ware Park, the Fanshawes' stately home, was quickly occupied by Parliamentary forces and the women folk found it necessary to find quarters elsewhere.

Sir Simon's wife and her child, the young Ferrers heiress, found sanctuary in the home of Lady Bedell at Hamerton in Huntingdonshire, and here in the pleasant, undisturbed district of Cromwell's birth they lived unaffected by the fortunes of war.

By 1653, the Fanshawes had become hunted men and, like so many Royalists, were forced to attempt most desperate measures to secure the means to survive. One such involved Sir William Lytton, a gallant old man and a former Fanshawe neighbour, in a desperate plan to enter Ware Park and, under the very noses of Cromwell's troops, secure some money and jewellery hidden for such an emergency. The attempt failed and Sir William was apprehended, and for a while his life hung in the balance.

It was then that Sir Simon Fanshawe discovered the means to alleviate all their financial problems. From his hide-out in Kent he sent messages to his brothers – Richard, then in exile in France, and the eldest of the family, Sir Thomas, who with his sixteen year old son, also named Thomas, was secreted in Ireland: the result being that all four risked their lives by emerging from their retreats and journeying across hostile land to meet in the village of Hamerton.

Once there Sir Simon's plans soon developed. With the assistance of

a priest named John Laycock, the twelve year old Ferrers heiress was married off to the sixteen-year-old youth. Once they had gained the power of attorney, the Fanshawes appointed two agents to act for them, and with the aid of an unscrupulous lawyer, Joshua Lomax, engineered the sale of the Ferrers property and fortune, converting the proceeds to their own needs. These transactions were conducted in such a manner that not even the slightest suspicion was aroused in Parliamentary quarters. The Fanshawes left Hamerton with their pockets well filled.

The years that followed brought much sadness to the very young wife. First her mother died and then soon after her benefactor Lady Bedell, an aged person, succumbed, leaving her completely on her own for the first time. So it was that Katherine, as she was named after her mother, returned to her heritage at Markyate. But only the great house and the park remained to her, and here, with a few servants to tend to her needs, she adopted the life of a recluse.

Legend has it that she met Ralph Chaplin, a farmer who lived on and worked a holding formerly owned by the Ferrers family. The house in which he lived, 'Buncers' still stands and overlooks Watling Street just south of Markyate. It is said that Chaplin augmented his income by robbing passing travellers, and in some way met and eventually introduced the Lady Katherine to the thrill of highway robbery. There is no evidence of this, but when Chaplin was finally caught in the act of robbing a baggage wagon, part of a cavalry unit, and was promptly despatched on the spot on Finchley Common, the terror of Markyate began.

From all accounts these senseless atrocities appear to be the result of a deranged mind. No attempt was made to rob, only to maim and more often to destroy. Houses were set on fire while inmates slept. Cattle were wantonly slaughtered in the fields. In one vicious attack Gunnell, the Caddington parish constable, in answering a summons at the dead of night, was murdered on his own door-step. There were many other people, travellers passing along Watling Street, who suffered a similar fate.

According to the legend, Lady Katherine's last exploit took place near St. Albans. A wagoner journeying from the city with supplies for an inn at Gustard Wood, near Wheathampstead, gave a lift to two men. These men climbed into the well of the vehicle and lay down among the bales and baggages. Evening light was falling and the wagon beginning to cross the No-Mans-Land common, when a rider suddenly appeared and, upon closing with the wagon, shot the wagoner from his box without the slightest warning. But one of the travellers fired back and saw the miscreant reel as though hit. The engagement ended with the rider racing away over the common.

The death of Lady Katherine Fanshawe may never be satisfactorily explained, but something happened in the June of 1660 that severely disturbed the noble family at Ware Park. The Fanshawes, like many other Royalists, had given unswerving service to Charles and had undergone many privations for his cause, and upon the restoration of the crown, looked for just rewards. But the King had limited funds and there arose much jealousy amongst the nobles, and the slightest hint of acrimony could have destroyed all hopes of the royal blessings.

The body of Lady Katherine was conveyed across Hertfordshire and buried at night in the parish church of St. Mary, Ware. It is perhaps significant that her remains were denied the right of internment in the Fanshawe family tomb, despite the fact that her husband subsequently became the most elevated member of this illustrious family.

When Lady Katherine died the name of the Markyate line of Ferrers died too, and the old mansion passed into other hands. But the stories of the young girl who died in most mysterious circumstances a few days after her twentieth birthday remain as fresh and fascinating as they were 300 years ago.

Doctor Goldfinger?

Gold has been sought by man since time immemorial. Some have searched the earth, failing or succeeding as fortune favoured. Others stayed at home – and tried to make it. And the world trembled, lest they did.

It is the accepted view in this atomic age that the manufacture of gold is practical, but it is not ever likely to become a commercial proposition as the costs of essential materials are excessive. But the importance of gold as a metal has not lessened and it remains as a standard of exchange throughout the world.

How different it would have been if Dr. John Kellerman had succeeded in manufacturing gold – a little more than a century ago – or did he succeed? No one knows. The mystery remains unanswered to this day.

Close to the present day boundaries of industrial Luton there stood a gloomy mansion. The house was almost hidden by a high surrounding wall. Intruders were not welcomed. On the wall were spikes, hurdles, broken glass and other devices to deter the uninvited. In the unkempt grounds beyond there lay, deviously hidden, scores of mantraps, so powerful as to sever a person's leg; only the gravelled drive was free, and this was patrolled day and night by armed guards.

Few ever passed through the massive gates, and those that did found the house barricaded like a fort. The windows on every floor were barred and shuttered. The place seemed deserted. Local folk spoke of it – as the abode of the devil.

Dr. Kellerman probably looked a person likely to be suspected of pursuing the black arts; he was more than six feet tall, slim in stature with long thin features to match. But far from being a magician, Dr. Kellerman was a scientist years before his day. He was born in the

West Indies. His father was a Prussian and a man of high repute while his mother was a princess in her own right, a Cree Indian of the extensive Algonquin nation. At an early age Kellerman came to Europe where, at his father's insistence, he studied at principal universities until 1811, when he came rather hurriedly to England. His life, he claimed, was in jeopardy.

Besides guards and trusted servants employed in his remote mansion, Kellerman had enlisted the services of eight highly skilled assistants. These worked in pairs on six hour shifts, day and night. The Doctor himself lived, worked and slept in one ground floor room while his men toiled over giant crucibles and ovens installed in other parts of the house. The mansion, in fact, was a secret and well-guarded laboratory.

Alarming reports reached Parliamentary ears in 1828, and as a result a high official was despatched to make further investigation. Sir Richard Phillips eventually traced Kellerman, and later visited the mansion at the Doctor's invitation. His report remains an official document to this day. Sir Richard drove up to the gates, revealed his identity to the guards, and after a short delay was escorted to the house. He noted the dilapidated state of the building and the broken windows, and the glass strewn about the remnants of a former lawn. They entered the Mansion from the rear and Sir Richard was led to a small room, where he was searched for concealed weapons and then left alone to await the coming of Dr. Kellerman.

Eventually he came, stooping slightly as he entered. The Doctor was polite, but very cautious and it was with some difficulty that Sir Richard got him to talk about his actual work. Then, apparently satisfied with the identity and purpose of his visitor, the Doctor relented.

Sir Richard found the man lived in fear. Agents of foreign powers were constantly endeavouring to enter the house. His life had been threatened. He himself was a walking arsenal. Kellerman showed Sir Richard that he carried no less than six pistols concealed in his various garments. The Doctor mentioned the broken windows, which Sir Richard had seen; these he claimed were the work of recent would-be intruders.

Kellerman stated that he could manufacture gold but he also admitted his discovery would bring disaster to many, disrupting the world's finance, and create tremendous power for the nation which possessed the secret. Kellerman told Sir Richard of staggering offers, which he had refused, for he felt certain that he would be murdered after revealing the process. For three hours Sir Richard talked to this strange man and eventually secured a proposal. Kellerman was prepared to supply gold to the British Government under certain conditions; one was constant armed protection.

Sir Richard agreed to put these proposals to his peers and then Kellerman conducted him into his own personal laboratory. Here he watched the Doctor perform, saw metals fuse under intense heat, and change. Then after a cooling operation, he was handed a huge nugget which appeared to be of pure gold. This Sir Richard was to present to Parliament in support of Kellerman's proposal.

Such revelations were staggering and seemingly undeniable, and yet Sir Richard was unable to determine whether this man was, indeed, a genius or a fraud, and it was the latter view that his superiors accepted upon receiving his report. So, a year later, when Kellerman sent a letter to the Prime Minister offering to clear the National Debt, it was disregarded and in a curt reply the Doctor was severely snubbed.

However, a short time later, the whole matter was reviewed. A small European country had suddenly revealed huge gold reserves. Hastily a deputation was despatched with orders to make amends for the previous insult and to re-open negotiations with Kellerman. The Government had accepted the possibility of manufacturing gold. But the house was empty. The Doctor and his assistant with all the scientific apparatus had gone. No one knew where, and despite almost desperate efforts by officialdom no trace has ever been found. True to form, the last of the alchemists, the man who claimed to hold the secret of gold, had disappeared from mortal ken.

The Leighton Wonder

Among the bric-a-brac at an auction held recently in Boston, Mass., U.S.A. was a large marble statue of Hercules which had previously adorned a Boston park for more than a century. A British visitor, a gentleman of Bedfordshire origin, recognised the figure as that for which Tom Tring, a Leighton Buzzard lad, posed in 1807. He purchased it and after many many years in the New World this stature is destined to return to the land of its origin.

But Tom Tring was not only an artist's model. True, he had a physique that stood out among men and had the fine, clear features likened to the Greek god. Tom Tring was the pride of Leighton Buzzard, a favourite of the Prince Regent, and one of the most promising prize-fighters of the age. Yet no man lost more in a single defeat than did Tom Tring.

Tom came from honest yeoman stock; his father was a respected tradesman in the town. Even in his childhood days young Tom had caused comments by his feats of strength in the Leighton market place. And as he grew older, more handsome and stronger, his father knew that his son was destined for greater things. At the age of nineteen, Tom went to London, and after several setbacks eventually obtained employment as a footman to His Royal Highness George August Frederick, the Prince of Wales.

It was a great stride in those days for a commoner of a little rural town to be employed by the greatest in the land. And Tom Tring knew it. It became his duty, with another Leighton lad, to transport His Royal Highness in a sedan chair. This was by no means simple, for the Prince was known for his weight and enormous proportions!

Tom's fine stature soon attracted attention and one of the Prince's associates sought permission for him to pose for a painting. Permission

was granted and the Bedfordshire lad became a model. Stripped to the waist, his great muscles rippling under a satin skin, Tom Tring soon became a feature of fashionable drawing rooms in Georgian London. The prince soon became aware of the interest his footman was causing, and promoted him to the rank of porter at his residence in Charlton House. Here the Leighton lad would stand on the stairway of the main entrance, armed with a great golden-headed mace and resplendent in a magnificent uniform. The Prince of Wales' porter rapidly became one of the sights of London. While those of his native town spoke of him as – OUR TOM. Yet Tom Tring was to climb even higher in the service of his Prince.

The Prince had many vices: one was gambling. He was known to have supported cock-fighting, bull-fighting and even badger-baiting, in fact anything likely to encourage a wager. He was perhaps the most ardent gambler of his time, even wagering thousands on the spin of a coin. At the time when the great bare-knuckle fights were frowned upon by the authorities, the Prince of Wales was one of their staunchest supporters.

So it was that Colonel Hanger, one of the Prince's band of sportsmen, noticed the upright young man from Leighton Buzzard in a different light. The result being that Tom Tring was sent by his royal master to the gymnasium of Tom Johnson, the champion prize-fighter of England. Tom had no particular enthusiasm for the fight game. He was quite satisfied with his present position, but to offend could mean the end of that. So Tom stuck out his chest, flexed his biceps and duly received the champion's approval.

"He'll make a grand fighter" Johnson reported. The Prince was delighted and set about arranging a match which saw Tom backed to the tune of five hundred guineas on his very first contest. The Prince's wager was accepted by Lord Malden who was to find a fighter who had no more than five fights, who he considered would thrash the Prince's man. Lord Malden found his man, an Irishman named Jacob Doyle, who stood six feet tall, weighed over fifteen stones and had two previous fights. His first opponent had been so battered that he was paralysed down one side of his body. Doyle's second victim retired after four rounds with three crushed ribs. Lord Malden was confident, but so was Colonel Hanger. Tom Tring was the guinea pig.

The fight took place in a little wood in the neighbourhood of Croydon. Tom met the fury of the Irishman's attack with a steady defence. For four rounds Doyle swung his great fists like flails, pummelling Tom's body until red wheals stood out on his satin skin. Then the Leighton lad seemed to have tired of the whole business. He suddenly bore into his opponent, swung one heavy blow to Doyle's head and the fight was over.

A few weeks later the jubilant Prince matched his man against a more experienced fighter – Jim Pratt. He went the same way as Doyle. So did Carrington, Watson and a celebrated pugilist known as the Iron Butcher. Tom beat Harry Norfolk, contender for the championship title, in record time, and had it not been for the condition set by Champion Johnson when he trained Tom that they should never meet in a ring, the Leighton man may have achieved the supreme honour. As it was it became necessary for the Prince to withdraw him from the eyes of the authorities.

Tom returned to his duty at Charlton House, bigger, prouder and more resplendent than ever. The young ladies of London clamoured at his feet, but Tom had an understanding with a Leighton lass; the outcome of a triumphant visit to his home town.

The Prince of Wales had many enemies. He and his fighter became the subject of wit. They were depicted in a well circulated broadsheet as a little fat man with horns and hoofs accompanied by a giant ape. The Prince was very annoyed, and he decided to show all England just how good his porter really was. So off Tom went again to the gym of Tom Johnson. Three months later it was agreed that he was ready to fight anyone in the country – except Tom Johnson. His royal master promptly backed him for a thousand guineas and sat back to wait the result. It was not long in coming. Ben Brain, who was considered the best fighter in England next to the champion himself, quickly took up the challenge and the match was made for the 18th December 1789.

All that morning roads to Dartford in Kent resounded from the gentries' carriages. All the sporting fraternity of London turned out to join a procession headed by His Royal Highness. It was a drab day, and the Prince was in a foul mood. There had been a re-appearance of the insulting broadsheet. Tom Tring stepped into the ring three stones lighter for his training. Even so he was well over fifteen stones. The champion himself stood in his corner and remarked, "One good blow and Tring could flatten a bullock."

Up they came, two wonderful specimens of manhood. Brain immediately went on the defensive. He'd heard enough about this Bedfordshire boy to be wary of those great fists. Tom kept up the attack, landing heavy blows upon his opponents body. Then, at a critical moment, he seemed to slip on the sodden grass. It was Brain's chance. He smashed a right hand to Tom's head and followed with a vicious left which gashed the cheek and sent Tom sprawling.

The Prince's porter stayed down and failed to come up to scratch in the required time. It was several minutes before Tom realised that he had lost but soon recovered enough to see his Royal master stamp off in a livid rage.

When poor Tom found his way back to Charlton House, he found himself sacked. No-one wanted him. And in Leighton Buzzard too. His lady love married a lesser man. And so it was that Tom Tring, once the pride of London, a prince's champion, and the hero of Leighton disappeared into the gloom of ignomy.

The Boy who came in Chains

It is a far cry from the depths of the Hertswold forest in north-west Germany to that pleasant village of Northchurch in Hertfordshire. But there is a strange story linking the districts which recalls an experiment with a child, an incident that caught the imagination of Georgian England . . . and almost cost the king his throne.

He was only a little lad, aged about twelve years when he was brought to England in a specially prepared cage in 1725. It had been several years earlier that the people of Hamelin, famed for the legendary piper, had reported that a small child was living an animal-like existence in the forest. They had made several attempts to catch him, but to no avail. News of these bizarre ventures caught the imagination of Britain's Germanic monarch, George I, and he launched an expedition to capture him. But the boy evaded their initial attempts with ease, and the monarch decided to take charge himself. He called up a large number of his crack Hanoverian troops, enlisted several skilled African animal-trackers and the tempo of the hunt increased. When the lad was eventually captured, contemporary reports stated that he fought with the fury of a wild beast. But as his captors were under strict orders not to injure him, they had to resort to the use of manacles and chains to secure him and to prevent the lad from injuring himself.

Once under the king's patronage, the wild boy was studied by some of Europe's most eminent doctors and scientists, but to little purpose. They reported that he was inclined to run on all fours, climbed trees with the agility of a monkey, and as far as they could see had existed on wild berries and on small animals which he apparently tracked down with amazing ease. He was of small stature, but seemed well nourished and astonishingly strong. Constant exposure, they reported, had apparently done him no harm, but his body was unclad except for the remains of a

linen cloth about his neck. The experts thought that the boy was the abandoned off-spring of some gypsy, or had wandered off into the forest at a very young age and been given up as lost by his parents.

No one came forward to claim the child, even though the king, simply revelling in the publicity, brought him to his royal residence and made much of him. But the lad sought every opportunity to escape, even seriously injuring himself on one occasion. The king's advisors suggested a fenced enclosure in more natural surroundings than those of the palace. So an acre of woodland was enclosed like a giant cage and the boy was released and became little more than George I's prize exhibition piece. But the king was not very popular, and his latest treatment of the child caused a great national outcry. The king, completely surprised by these events, made a desperate attempt to restore what little popularity he once had. He enlisted several famous tutors and once again moved the lad into the royal household. It was to display his personal interest that the king chose the name of Peter for his charge. But Peter showed no sign of responding to his teachers and despite exhaustive efforts on their part the lad still could not utter an intelligent word, or accept even the rudiments of civilized life.

Peter had become an embarrassment and the king, very conscious of the mounting hostility towards him, looked about in desperation to rid himself of the boy. An avenue presented itself in the person of one of Queen Charlotte's attendants. So it was that the Wild Boy came to live in Northchurch in the care of a Mrs Tichbourne, who found her monarch's generous allowance most rewarding.

Whether Mrs Tichbourne found her charge more difficult than she imagined is not known, but after a very short spell the boy was placed with a farmer named Fenn. And for the very first time the wild boy apparently found something in common with a fellow human, for he followed the farmer wherever he went. Peter seemed content in these rural surroundings. He wandered at will and seemed to be able to communicate with the farm animals and with the wild-life that abounded in those parts.

Then, one day Peter seemed to disappear. The farmer and his servants scoured the district in the hope of finding him. Even the king offered a large reward for his return to Northchurch and although the wild boy's description was publicised throughout the neighbouring counties, it was of no avail. It seemed as though the wild boy had gone for ever.

Then came startling news from Norwich. A great fire had swept the city, destroying many buildings including the local prison, known as the Norwich Bridewell. And all the imprisoned occupants had seized the opportunity to escape, except one man, who had been locked up a few days earlier as a vagrant. This fellow amazed everyone by his indifference to the danger by standing and staring at the flames while the building burnt about him, until finally he was forcefully removed. It was Peter. He had wandered across England, some said following an animal instinct, to reach a district nearer to his native haunts.

He was brought back to Northchurch, and once again allowed to roam freely about the farm, but Peter never tried to escape again. Mr Fenn, the farmer, claimed that this was caused by Peter having discovered that there was a vast expanse of water between him and his old haunts, and he had, animal-like, resigned himself to his fate. Nevertheless, Farmer Fenn had a leather collar fastened about his neck, suitably inscribed, in case his charge should ever wander again.

As he grew older the wild boy lost much of the suspicion that he formerly had of those about him, but he displayed a passion for music and would dance and caper about whenever a musical instrument was played within his hearing. At this stage he had abandoned all desire to climb trees, and walked normally. But nothing could persuade him to work, and whenever he could Peter preferred to sleep in the fields, eating berries and fruit from the orchards and hedgerows. He ended his days peacefully at Northchurch, and today, close to the south porch of the village church, a small headstone marks his resting place.

The Common Crime

Had it been possible for two Bedfordshire boys, long since dead, to have been present at a recent sitting of a county juvenile court, they most certainly would have expressed violent resentment. Resentment not directed against the modern outlook towards young offenders, but of the unwavering severity of their own times.

The occasion was commonplace, too much so, by modern standards. In the well of the court stood a schoolboy. He was a pink-cheeked youngster, well nourished, educated and clothed. He had been arrayed before the magistrates on a charge of wilfully damaging a hayrick, setting it on fire and causing a loss of several hundred pounds to its owner.

The boy pleaded guilty to this charge, and the magistrates, exercising a degree of leniency undreamed of a hundred years ago, placed him on probation. But the case did not pass without incident. For the boy's father, in pleading for his son, described the misdeed as a 'schoolboy prank'; a view which caused a sharp reprimand from the magistrates.

But both of those earlier Bedfordshire lads would have had one thing in common with the modern delinquent. For young Robert Addington and the even younger Robert Reeve had also been charged during their lives with destroying a hayrick. But the comparison ended there. For them, there was no special court set apart from the atmosphere of an adult criminal session. Neither had they persons to speak for them in their defence, although they both maintained their innocence to the end. Poor, homeless vagrants as they were, Addington and Reeve provided excellent subjects upon whom the law could demonstrate its severity as a deterrent to others.

Robert Addington was born in the Bedfordshire village of Wilstead in 1815. His parents, who, it appears, were never other than poverty-stricken during the greater part of their lives, had nevertheless increased their brood by the time the boy had reached the age of seventeen to seven other children.

It may have been through force of circumstance – the survival of the majority – or perhaps a mere domestic upheaval that caused the boy's expulsion from the parental home. No one knows. But the boy was forced to fend for himself, living as best he could in the fields and lanes about Wilstead, and he very soon became subject to discrimination, reaping the blame for all the mishaps in the district.

Then one day Robert Addington was seized. A hayrick situated in one of the fields which he was known to frequent had been burned down. The owner, only too eager to place guilt in human hands, accused the young outcast and reported the matter. Accordingly the lad was hauled off to Bedford and there uncerimoniously deposited in the dark, dank depths of the county gaol.

After a lapse of several months, Robert Addington was eventually brought to trial. It was a short sitting, for the justices were not inclined to spend much of their time considering such a matter. Despite the fact that the accused vehemently professed his innocence and there was no conclusive evidence to prove otherwise, he was found guilty and sentenced accordingly. In the summer of 1832, Robert Addington, miserable, friendless creature that he was, faced his maker at the end of a rope within the confines of Bedford gaol.

Twenty five years later, another boy of even more tender years found himself in similar circumstances in Luton. In matters concerning twelve year old Robert Reeve, and the affair that brought him before the justices in 1857, there is even more evidence of lack of sympathy. For Reeve, like Addington before him, was virtually a waif of the streets, and, as it seems, from no fault of his own. For, according to the records Robert Reeve was born in Church Street, Luton, and was bereft of his mother's care while still a mere toddler. Her sudden death appears to have affected his father's outlook on life. For he became a drunk, committed offence after offence, and duly spent many years behind bars.

So it was that Robert Reeve was forced to beg at a very early age, even stealing to survive. He soon became known to local tradesmen, who from time to time had cause to bemoan the loss of a cheese, a ham, or a loaf of bread. In consequence no one liked him, and even more tragically nobody seems to have had any concern for him.

According to all reports, a woman living in the Brache farm house, now the site of residential dwellings in Park Street, one evening noticed whiffs of smoke issuing from behind some adjacent stables. A hayrick

46

close to the building had caught fire, and immediately she ran into the adjoining road, calling for help. Some distance away she saw a small boy who came running at her call and plunged into the stables, freeing the frightened animals and with her aid leading them to safety.

Meanwhile the smoke attracted several other people who also offered their assistance. Among these newcomers was a man who lodged at the nearby 'Goat' public house, and who, for some reason best known to himself, suggested before the crowd that had now gathered about the farmhouse that the culprit who caused the fire of the hayrick in the first instance might well be Reeve, as he was first on the scene.

Whether or not this fellow held a grudge against the lad was never even queried, even though he subsequently appeared in court to testify against Reeve. Also a newspaper report on the affair reveals that on the day following the fire Reeve was supposed to have spoken to another fellow who was in the crowd outside the farmhouse that day, and admitted to him that he had caused the outbreak. Even this fellow, when questioned in court, admitted that the boy had stolen a loaf of bread and some cheese from his house on the day of the fire.

The enormity of the situation must have overawed the twelve year old as he listened to the charge of which he was accused. Timidly, but unwaveringly, he denied setting fire to the hayrick. However, he did admit the theft of the food which he claimed happened several days before the day of the fire, and that the owner had forgiven him. Reeve claimed he had been starving at the time.

The justices were not impressed by the boy's admissions, nor, in fact, by anything that he had to say in his defence. It seems that they were satisfied with the evidence, flimsy and bigotted as it was, that Reeve was guilty. The very fact that he had purchased a box of Lucifers from a shop some days prior to the incident was to their mind a major factor proving his guilt. So without much delay the verdict of guilty was reached and young Robert Reeve was sentenced to six years penal servitude.

Such were the conditions in gaols of those times that very few, other than those endowed with the strongest of constitutions ever survived their sentence. So it is not surprising that there is no evidence of Robert Reeve outliving his. Like that of Addington, young Reeve's world was one of hunger, misery, viciousness and precious little sympathy.

Beyond the Headlights

There is one incident in everyone's life that is most readily recalled. For Jock Cameron, one of the most successful officers in H.M.'s service, that occurred when he began his working life as a modest van boy. Fortune favoured him when he was teamed with driver Ted Bates. But the last ride together completely changed his outlook on life.

It had been raining all day, and as they headed for home the very skies seemed to burst. They had delivered their load and were returning empty, eager for Christmas Eve on the following day.

Ted Bates was already in a festive mood, despite the rain. He was looking forward to a reunion with Bert, his brother-in-law, and his missus, who had promised to visit them over Christmas.

'Always got on with Bert,' he mused.

'Salt of the earth. . old Bert.' Driver Bates chuckled as he fondly recalled their last meeting, and how they had staggered home after that binge last Christmas, and how they had to weather the storm of female tongues. For sisters they might be . . . but when his Jenny and Bert's Elsie got together . . . well . . . as they say . . . hell hath no fury like female tongues. Ted Bates' grin broadened as he peered into the night.

They had just cleared Ryton when Ted Bates glanced at his van boy on the adjoining seat. Young Jock had been very quiet during the last half hour, and Ted thought that unusual, for the boy was normally an incessant chatter-box. But he grinned again as he found the lad curled up in a deep sleep . . . Then, looking back to the road again, he stifled a shout and frantically spun the steering wheel, smashing down on the brake pedal with all his might. The great lorry swung crazily, then slipped and slithered to a halt, blocking the entire south-bound traffic lane.

A little white face had suddenly appeared on the wet tarmac before him. The headlights caught the vestige of a blue dress as the child threw up two tiny hands in protection before disappearing beneath the wheels of the thundering lorry.

Jock Cameron came to his senses on the floor of an empty cab. The driver's door yawned open, and he had to blink in the glare of oncoming headlights, slowing as they approached. But where was Ted Bates? The thought raced through his mind as he threw open the near-side door and jumped down onto a wet, grassy bank. The road behind was already jammed with traffic. Line after line, unable to pass, their headlights illuminated the scene as if it was day.

Ted Bates was crawling under the lorry and emerged only to plunge into the depths of an adjoining drainage ditch. Then a host of shadowy figures came racing upon the scene. It all seemed a horrid nightmare to young Jock, and when Bates screamed "I've run a kid over. Look in the ditch! Quick," the van boy only wished it was. All he could do was to splutter, "But how? Where?" But Ted ignored Jock, as a tall uniformed figure emerged to confront him. In a moment one police officer was calmly directing an extensive search, while another directed the traffic. But search as they all might, no trace could be found, and even Bates had to agree that there were no marks of contact to be found on the lorry. But he was adamant that he had run down a small child.

Bemused by it all, young Jock had further cause for concern when he saw Ted Bates in a heated argument with the police officers before being almost forcibly bundled into a patrol car. But he was not left to wonder long.

"Get back in the cab." It was the tall uniformed man again. "I'm going to drive for a bit."

Young Jock hesitated.

"Just do as you're told. Your mate's alright . . . needs a break . . . that's all. Now get up there or I'll leave you behind."

Sergeant Beck knew how to manage the huge vehicle, for they pulled away smartly and were soon overhauling the patrol car.

"Did you see anything back there?" Beck's eyes were rivetted on the road as he spoke.

"No . . . . . I was asleep," said Jock.

"Your mate . . . . . is he usually like that?"

The vivid picture of Ted Bates crawling under the lorry flooded Jock Cameron's mind.

"No . . . but then . . .", the lad hesitated.

"Then what?" demanded Beck.

"Well . . . Ted's never run anyone down before."

"Before?" Beck challenged. "But you didn't see anything this time

50

either . . . did you? Asleep you said."

Young Jock was lost for words, but he felt a sudden chill run down his spine.

They had travelled some twenty miles or so when the police car ahead signalled and pulled into a layby. Sergeant Beck drove in behind, and without further ado, dismounted, and strode over to it. Minutes later,

Ted Bates reappeared and with the sergeant in close attendance, walked back to the lorry and climbed up behind the wheel once more.

"You're sure that you feel alright?" The officer queried. But Bates merely nodded and drove the lorry on to the highway again.

Young Jock had many questions to ask of his driver. But a quick glance at Bates was enough to stifle them. For he appeared strangely tense and a worried frown puckered his face. So they sat in silence as the huge wagon lumbered into Towcester's long and narrow High Street. The place was crowded with people, filling the pavements and all the brilliantly lit windows as Christmas shopping reached its peak. White-faced, Ted Bates began to thread his way through. Cars parked on both sides restricted his passage, while shadows darting from side to side kept him on edge. Suddenly Bates jammed on the brakes, and again the van boy was pitched uncerimoniously on to the floor. But not before he had seen a tiny tot, desperately chased by its mother, emerge from behind a parked car to run in front of them. The great lorry lurched, and ground to a halt within inches of the child. The danger was quickly cleared, but Ted Bates remained seemingly frozen at the wheel, unable to move a muscle.

Jock Cameron looked frantically about him as the traffic in both directions had come to a sudden halt. The High Street was jammed with vehicles. It was then that Sergeant Beck made a reappearance. He forced his way into the cab, pushed the stricken Bates over on to the startled van boy and drove the lorry safely through.

Ted Bates had recovered from his daze long before Sergeant Beck handed over to him on the outskirts of Dunstable. He switched off the engine and looked Bates squarely in the face. "Now look. This is as far as I'm going! You understand?" As he spoke, a patrol car arrived alongside. "You have less than six miles to go, and now get it in that thick head of yours . . ." Beck seemed merciless. "You did not run anyone down, but . . . how can I put it?" the Sergeant was groping for words. "You actually did see a child on the road back there. But it is nearly five years since she was killed . . and . . .". Beck hesitated again. "Her ghost . . . if that's what you wish to call it . . . has appeared on that spot eight times since. And every time the driver concerned was so keyed up . . . just like you . . . and avoided running down another child later on by the very skin of his teeth. Like it or not . . . we have records to prove it."

Ted Bates drove the lorry on into Luton that night, parked it in its usual place in the company garage, locked up, and without a word to his van boy, walked away as if in a dream. He never drove a vehicle again.

Friendless Lane

Friendless is an uncommon name for a by-way, even in a county given to unusual place-names. Yet for the last two hundred years, a narrow country lane linking Flamstead with the hamlet of Cheveralls Green in west Hertfordshire has borne this unenviable title.

Early records refer to the road as Cheveralls Lane, but like so many of our quaint English place-names, common reference to a particular spot has determined its present name, which many local folk prefer to pronounce as "frindles".

However, there was a far different reason for the tag 'Friendless', for, if local legend has any relation to fact, a small but rather noticeable mound by the roadside is the burial place of a particularly unsavoury character, a man who died absolutely friendless.

Two hundred years ago an increase in crime brought about a wave of indignation, and several reforms were introduced. One scheme sought to induce people to inform on suspects and to act in a manner similar to that of the infamous "bounty hunter" of the American West. Upon conviction of such a suspected person the informer was awarded a certificate which in effect exempted him from the then cumpulsory, unpaid and therefore very unpopular parish duties which more often than not involved great hardship upon rich and poor alike.

The law allowed the recipient to dispose of this award for financial gain should he wish, and such was the demand for the 'Tyburn ticket', as it was called, that large sums often changed hands. The laxity of regulations concerning this particular reform allowed the emergence in society of an obnoxious type known as the 'ticket seeker', people who were not averse to the submitting of false evidence to gain their ends.

These tyrants were particularly feared in small communities, and in Markyate, a few miles north of Flamstead, an innkeeper, who augmented his income by informing, ruled the village like a feudal lord.

Abel Goodyear pursued his despicable practice whenever he could. The unfortunate wayfarer was easy prey, but Goodyear was not above 'framing' a case against members of his own community. For he knew that the average villager had neither the means nor the ability to defend himself ably in the courts, so the rascally innkeeper would lay charges against those whom he disliked, and the law . . . in its blindness . . . worked for him.

There was, however, one who was as popular among his fellows as Goodyear was abhorred, and Fred Fox, a hostler and a native of Flamstead, unfortunately came into Goodyear's employ. This happy-go-lucky character was in the habit of borrowing a donkey from one aged associate, and a cart from another. With this he contrived to add to his meagre income when the occasion arose. And of course, Goodyear was aware of this, for when Fox subsequently terminated his service with him and took employment with a rival Markyate innkeeper, Abel's fury knew no bounds. He swore that Fox would rue the day, and a few weeks later the Flamstead man really did have cause for concern . . .

For one morning Fred Fox was arrested in the village High Street and with very little ceremony hauled off to Hertford jail, there to languish until his trial. Before the justices, Fox learned to his horror that he was charged with the theft of the donkey which he had been in the habit of borrowing. A few hours before his last use of the animal Abel Goodyear had purchased it, and what was more, taken care to keep knowledge of the transaction from the unfortunate hostler. For he recalled that the original owner, old Tom Redman, had been in such a drunken stupor and could not utter a word when he called upon him, as was his custom before taking the donkey from its paddock. Unwittingly Fred Fox had walked into Goodyear's dastardly snare.

However, Fox's disposition stood him in good stead, for, although the cost was heavy upon them, the risk of incurring Goodyear's wrath being very real, eight of his friends had made the journey to speak in his defence. And that they had done so was not lost upon the justices, who, upon hearing the evidence of the former owner, dismissed the case but soundly reprimanded Goodyear and warned him as to his future conduct. But this did not deter the innkeeper, for a few days later he was again plotting Fox's downfall.

Among the many dubious characters who were known to consort with Goodyear was William Conn, a particularly villainous vagabond. The plot was for Conn to waylay the hostler on his homeward journey through Cheveralls lane. Conn was to injure his victim so as to provide an example to others not to cross the innkeeper, who, having been

publicly exposed, felt the need to restore his prestige.

The plan might have succeeded but for Goodyear's overbearing nature. The very thought of witnessing such a beating greatly appealed to him, so much so that at the last moment he decided that he would indeed watch Fox being attacked. He hurried along the lane, and in the gathering gloom came upon Conn. That miscreant thought it was Fox and struck a savage blow to the head. Again the cudgel smote Goodyear, smashing him to the ground, where the blows continued to rain down upon his crumpled body.

Abel Goodyear paid the supreme penalty for his dastardly scheme in Cheveralls Lane. His body was later discovered and Conn, a simple-minded fellow, was so confused on discovering his mistake, that he gave himself up and related the whole story.

Such was the curious outlook of the law of those days that Conn was apparently sentenced to a short term of imprisonment, the view being that he had unwittingly served in ridding society of a criminal. So legend has it that Goodyear was buried like a common highwayman at the scene of his intended crime. And from that day on a little mound by the roadside gave birth to a new name –

Friendless Lane.

The Day the Crack Whip Lost His Crown

Humphrey Spry was a Markyate man and the populace of that small Hertfordshire village, having little else to boast about, made much of it. For Spry had emerged from their impoverished midst to become a champion in a highly competitive field. At the peak of his career the Markyate man was recognised as the 'Crack Whip on Watling Street' an accolade, greatly coveted, which signified that he was the finest coach driver of the day.

For horse drawn transport was reaching its zenith and the coaching system, despite ruinous highways, had reached near perfection. However, fierce competition between the various concerns was often reflected in the driving by rival whips, and reckless racing often brought about disastrous consequences. Speed was the key note. One Markyate innkeeper who contracted to supply fresh horses for changeovers, found he was allowed but four minutes to accomplish the task and was subject to a fine for every minute taken in excess.

Spry as champion enjoyed an enormous advantage over other drivers in so much as his services were always in demand. Markyate folk basked in his glory and very few travellers pausing in the village ever departed without some glowing account of his exploits being pressed upon them. Yet, in the course of time, it was these very admirers who unwittingly caused Spry's decline and also attracted such humiliation upon themselves that they became the laughing stock of the country.

It was the autumn of 1842, shortly after George Stephenson's 'Rocket' had attracted a multitude of sightseers, many Markyate folk among them, to a railway embankment near Tring. On that day Stephenson savoured his finest hour, but for those whose livelihood depended on the horse and horse-drawn transport it sounded an ominous warning – and one that was not lost upon them. For already

there had been a marked decline on the roads and as trade fell so did the demand for horse fodder and all the kindred trades associated with the horse. But to make matters worse speculators in London were bent on challenging the established coach concerns with the introduction of a steam-powered coach. And since Markyate was situated on the lucrative London and Birmingham route, the village had to be negotiated on the inaugural run.

Markyate had special hazards. Even in the 19th century its long and narrow High Street which formed part of the Watling Street posed a serious traffic problem. In places this thoroughfare was barely sixteen feet wide and on market days the highway was even further restricted by numerous stalls, herds of cattle, local vehicles and milling pedestrians. Even so, through this dangerous bottleneck came a daily stream of traffic. Long strings of pack-horses, still forming the major goods carrier, plying with heavy wagons, some pulled by as many as eight horses. Then there were the coaches. No less than ninety fast passenger vehicles passed through Markyate each day. On market days even the most reckless of drivers took good care to negotiate the place at a walking pace. For Markyate had an appalling accident record.

But all this was unknown to the steam-coach engineer as he

approached Markyate at the height of its market-day bustle. That worthy fully expected his vehicle to be the subject of wonder and admiration as had been the case in places already traversed.

Squire Coppin records that the steam coach entered the village like a visitation from hell. For amidst a dense cloud of smoke and showers of sparks the strange ponderous vehicle lumbered into sight. Its great wheels hurled loose stones against the village walls with frightening force, while the thunder of its passage drowned all other sounds. Then, before anyone could appreciate the danger, every horse, regardless of which vehicle was attached to it, made a bolt up the street in the opposite direction. Chaos ruled as the fleeing animals smashed everything in their path while panic-stricken Markyate folk sought refuge where they could. The steam-coach engineer, dumbfounded by the scene, hastily increased speed and departed in the wake of the fleeing animals.

Few had escaped without some loss but, while many nursed minor injuries, no one had been killed or seriously injured. However, local pride had received a severe knock. Squire Coppin had been thrown from his favourite horse as it bolted with the rest, and the vicar, who was making a dignified passage in his pony-cart, had had the galling humiliation of finding himself deposited unceremoniously in the garden of his most vociferous non-conformist opponent. But all local grievances were forgotten as Markyate folk laboured long into the night clearing their High Street and assessing the damage. It was not enough that steam power was threatening their livelihood; it seemed also as though their very homes were in jeopardy too. So it was that Markyate folk, united as never before, decided on a plan to halt the stride of progress.

Three days later, after a substitute engineer had been secured – the original swearing that he would never drive through Markyate again – the steam coach began its south-bound journey. News got through that Markyate was to be traversed at night to avoid further trouble and, to ensure this, the coach was to stop in Dunstable, five miles north, until nightfall.

This suited the vengeful villagers ideally for, as the evening shadows descended, a body of lusty men flaunted the law by digging a huge trench spanning the Watling Street. The site was carefully chosen. A mile north of Markyate at the junction of Kensworth Turn, a slight downhill slope encouraged south-bound traffic to accelerate through a sharp bend where the road was shrouded by overhanging trees. In the darkness the gaping hole was barely noticeable and even the most wary of travellers would have failed to have seen it until it was much too late.

Earlier that evening the steam-coach had duly arrived in Dunstable, where its passengers took respite, possibly in the Sugar Loaf, while the engineer tended his vehicle, surrounded by a large crowd. It was upon this gathering that Humphrey Spry had had cause to cast a withering look. For the Crack Whip of Watling Street had driven into Dunstable and had not attracted so much as the slightest salutation. His dignity damaged, Spry had observed the steam coach and the crowd about it with great disdain. In a loud voice he hailed the engineer and his conveyance with some choice epithets which brought that worthy across the road in a fit of fury. Battle would have ensued there and then had it not been for the passengers of both vehicles. They chose to debate the virtues of their respected carriages with a wager in mind rather than a bout of fisticuffs. A race was proposed between Dunstable and Markyate, the highway over the five miles being considered wide enough between these points to attempt such a contest. A prize of twenty guineas was offered and both drivers, fully appreciating the importance of the occasion, readily accepted the challenge.

Excitement reached fever pitch as the two coaches finally lined up in the main street. Almost at the last moment the passengers of both vehicles decided that the hazards of such a journey were too great, and declined to travel. Then both guards signified that they were also in accord, and came off too. So it was left to Spry alone to carry the prestige of all horse-drawn vehicles while upon the steamer's engineer rested the laurels of a new invention assailing the established realm.

There are several accounts of this fantastic race enshrined in the legends of the coaching era, all to the acute embarrassment of Markyate folk. But it appears that Spry's magnificent four-in-hand, fresh beasts put on at Dunstable and chosen from a host of animals offered by almost every stable in the town, swept into an early lead. But on cresting the Half Moon hill the steamer began to narrow the gap. Very soon Spry was acutely conscious of the pursuing vehicle and looking back, experienced the first doubts of his undertaking. Showers of sparks belched from the smoke stack cascading over the darkened hedgerows while the engineer, just discernable amid a thundering, pulsating shadow, seemed to be clinging on for his life. Nearer and nearer came the steamer until Spry, now fully convinced of his folly, turned his attention once again to his horses to find to his dismay that they were now out of control. They too had sensed the monster behind and were hauling their coach in headlong flight.

In the mid-1800s the Turnpike Trust, headed by Thomas Pickford, founder of the carrier firm and a Markyate man, had reason to be proud. They had not only fashioned the best section on the entire length of Watling Street but in 1839 had re-sited the Half Moon toll gate with a fine new gate and house at Beech Row. The man in charge, Jeremiah Goodyear, was considered one of the most zealous collectors in England, and for Humphrey Spry that night this posed an alarming problem.

For Spry now knew that he could not stop his terrified animals and had even greater doubt about the ability of the engineer behind him controlling his vehicle. The toll gate would be closed and the thought of the pending disaster caused Spry to consider the risk of leaping from the bounding coach. But Jeremiah had heard the roar of the approaching steamer and upon spying the pillar of sparks in the darkness, abandoned all sense of duty. He opened the gate and quickly retired to a place of safety. The horse-drawn coach raced through unscathed, much to Spry's relief, but the steamer, at that moment in the process of overtaking, was hugging the road edge and struck the gate mechanism, tearing it from its foundation and demolishing the front of Goodyear's house.

The collision slowed the ponderous vehicle enough to give Spry time to gather his wits. And as he raced for the Kensworth Turn he felt that victory was his, even more so as his team responded to the reign on the sharp bend beyond. A quick glance behind gave him extra satisfaction for he saw the steamer apparently out of control, fail to take the bend and go hurling through the hedge and bury itself in the soft ground beyond. Seconds later Humphrey found himself amid a deluge of splintering wood and struggling horses as his coach came to grief in the saboteurs' trench!

A local historian, writing of the incident some years later, declared that almost every Markyate craftsman was enlisted that night in a desperate attempt to repair the coach. And most of all they wanted to keep the incident a secret. Even Spry saw the wisdom of this. But it was not to be. The story leaked out and was related wherever travellers met and it took nearly fifty years before Markyate folk could live it down. And as for the purely experimental steam coaches – they ran for less than a year!

The Miracle Boy

Within yards of Luton's Town Hall, at the very hub of this ever-expanding community, a local man earned his daily bread. Modest as his calling might have been, George Fisher, a newspaper vendor, was just as much a part of Luton as that noble edifice which towered above him. He was known to thousands, casually and most times indifferently, as a trader who served their needs from the sheaves of newspapers draped over his arm. Yet, to a few who knew him well, he was . . . Georgie – the Miracle Boy, an unparalleled example of the power of Faith Healing.

I knew Georgie well. Arthur Hailey, the Lutonian whose writings are renowned world-wide, was well aware of him. For we were all classmates at the Surrey Street School. But Georgie was different. He was brought and carried from the classrooms in an invalid chair, for Georgie was paralysed in all four limbs and had been so since birth.

We boys used to pity him, but sympathy was of little use to a lad doomed to a wheel-chair while all about him echoed with the virility and enthusiasm of life. At playtime Georgie was the lone figure in the classroom, and at night his was the ashened face pressed so eagerly against the window-pane . . . as the world went by.

Then came the miracle. It happened in 1929, when what is now the Seymour Road, part of the Brache district of Luton, was a mere collection of curb stones thrown roughly over the pleasant meadows of Brache Farm, the home of John Seymour. News had spread like wild fire throughout the school, a large tent had appeared on the site. So, thinking it was a circus, practically the entire school turned up on the opening night.

But it was not a circus. There was none of the usual pomp and pageantry about this tent. Instead at the very entrance there stood stark and sobering . . . a large wooden cross. It was the travelling mission of a

movement led by Pastor Edward Jefferies, probably the greatest spiritual leader of the age.

As we all stood there, dubious whether to join the queue, a familiar figure came into sight. It was Georgie, seated in his wheel-chair, smiling radiantly as his doting mother, resplendent in a white apron, trundled him along. In the tent they went, and we boys tarried no longer. So it was that Georgie's class-mates witnessed what surely must have been one of the most moving ceremonies ever enacted in Luton.

After a spell of communal singing, there came prayers, in which the entire assembly over two thousand strong with several hundred more outside, took part. On a small stage arrayed before the preacher's pulpit a number of sick and infirm people began to gather. Georgie was among them, a little bewildered and certainly very scared. It was to him that the slightly built, pleasant-faced Pastor Jefferies stepped.

There was utter silence in that marquee as he placed his hands on the boy's head. A moment of suspense as the Pastor murmured earnestly. Then, taking the boy's two hands, he drew Georgie from his chair. Still speaking directly to the boy, the Pastor got Georgie on to his feet, then stepped back suddenly, leaving the boy standing, unsupported and unaided. It was the first time that anyone had seen Georgie Fisher stand alone; his mother was in tears and we all watched aghast.

Pastor Jefferies was still talking, firmly, confidently and convincingly. Georgie responded. He took a step forward – the first in his life. Then another, and yet another. But this was not all. The minister grasped the boy's paralysed arms and lifted them high above Georgie's head, and loosed his grip.

Georgie moved first one limb, then the other, up and down and then up again, while the entire assembly gasped with amazement.

George Fisher pushed his wheel chair home that night as many Luton people can testify, and the next morning there was a new boy in the playground. One who played with the joyousness of a new life gained in the shadow of the cross.

The Thief in the Night

A low cloud hung over Britain on the night of September 2nd, 1916, but thousands had gathered, many disturbed from sleep to gaze anxiously at the drama enacted in the skies above. The guns on the Pegsdon heights had ceased to bellow but the search-lights were joined by the stabbing fingers of the battery on Offey Hill. And more from Ley Green and Kimpton illuminated the scene. They had caught a zeppelin and despite the clouds were tracing its every movement. But the beams had revealed another shape, a small fragile looking aeroplane circling in attack.

On the outbreak of World War One, Germany was the sole nation in the world with military airships and two years later such was their considered need that fifty eight were in service and no aircraft in use by any of the allied forces had been able to combat them. And on that September evening sixteen of Germany's most vaunted airships had left for a mass attack on the midland counties. By 2-00 am, L16 was over St. Albans, L32 was nearing Tring and L21 was looming above Hitchin, caught in the Pegsdon search-lights and held.

In pre-war days the development of the airship had captured the imagination of many, but with the outbreak of war it had become an object of dread. The thief in the night, some newspapers dubbed it, so silent and stealthy was its approach. In fact it was the gondola, containing the bomb aimer and wound down from the parent ship to within a few feet of selected targets that raised the earliest warning of a zeppelin's presence. Folk were astounded by the feat, but not panic stricken as the Germans hoped they would. For their object was to demoralise civilian population and that was not to be.

But at last on the borders of Herts and Beds one of Britain's antiquated

aircraft had encountered an enemy airship.

Three hours earlier young Leefe Robinson, flying a BE2c aeroplane, had taken off from a farm near Hornchurch and begun a night patrol on a selected area. It was a dark night and the pilot knew that the chances of detecting an enemy craft were very remote. Much depended upon the ground forces detecting a marauder and illuminating him with search-lights. For two hours he flew back and forth on his allotted area and saw nothing. Then about 1-00 am he saw a pool of light concentrated in the clouds to the north of London and turned to investigate. His craft was far too slow and sluggish in the climb to intercept but he glimpsed the silver cigar shape as it disappeared in a cloud formation. Incensed by failure Leefe Robinson was about to return to his Hornchurch base when he noticed another pool of light further to the north. Immediately he headed towards it. A zeppelin had been caught in search-lights above Hatfield and was being held by a succession of other batteries. Leefe Robinson quickly put his aircraft into a shallow dive to gain speed and very soon found himself close to the enemy ship but several hundred feet below it. There was one hazard that he had not reckoned with. The Pegsdon guns were blasting away, and hidden in darkness the BE2c was in grave danger of being hit. For the most part the anti-aircraft shells were bursting below and to the right of the zeppelin and an attack under these circumstances was suicidal and Leefe Robinson was forced to swing away. Then one beam picked him up, outlining his frail craft and following him as he steadily climbed ahead of the airship. The guns ceased and a crimson Very light lit the sky. Leefe Robinson knew that the gunners had given him his chance, and he pressed home his first attack. But the zeppelin gunners were also aware and were prepared for his pass below, and although bullets from his Lewis gun raked the vessel from stem to stern he saw the fabric ripped off his upper wing as the enemy fired back. With his airspeed falling alarmingly, Leefe Robinson drove in at the right side and had to bank sharply away to avoid further damage. From a safe distance Leefe Robinson studied the giant, now held in the grasp of a dozen search-lights. The zeppelin seemed unhindered but had reversed its course and was now heading for the cover of a cloud formation. Disappointed that he had not inflicted serious damage in his passes at the airship, Leefe Robinson elected to use the last of his ammunition in an attack on the giant tail section. But the enemy were ready for him and the young pilot saw men scramble along the cat-walk and man machine guns on the very top of the zeppelin. He would have to brave a barrage to press home his attack. But he was determined, and he would use their own tactics against them. The BE2c was a few feet behind and above the airship as it nosed into the cloud-bank. And as the cloud gradually shrouded the giant in mist, screening its gunners, Leefe Robinson made his attack. He swooped down, exhausted his magazine into the faint outlines of the great fins, and banked swiftly away. For a few seconds nothing happened. Then the giant tail began to glow, illuminating the cloud, and suddenly flames burst through the entire envelope. The zeppelin seemed to topple and then plunge earthwards like a blazing comet. It crashed on farm-land near the Hertfordshire village of Cuffley, where it burned for two hours.

Leefe Robinson was awarded the Victoria Cross for his daring that night and the L21's fate signalled the end of enemy airship supremacy over Britain, and subsequent victories saw the zeppelin banished from British skies.

*   *   *

Lt. William Leefe Robinson V.C. was born in India. He was twenty one when he brought L21 down. It was the first zeppelin destroyed on British soil and it was the anniversary of his becoming a pilot. Later, as a flight leader in new Bristol fighters, he sought and engaged the famous German ace, Baron von Richthofen. He died in December 1918 and was buried in the churchyard of All Saints, Stanmore.

Old Lal

Thomas Pickford frowned when he heard the news. There had been another crash. The bodies of the guard on the Manchester coach and two of the passengers on the London-bound vehicle were lying in the Sun Inn yard. But that was not all; a Markyate hostler had been involved and the collision had cost him both legs. Labordor Hall, or Old Lal as he was familiarly known, had been changing horses for the Woburn coach outside the Sun when the speeding Manchester coach struck the stationary vehicles. And Pickford knew it was yet another instance of reckless driving, and he felt responsible. For his foremost ambition to expand his carrier concern throughout the nation had seen him become chairman of the Turn Pike Trust and he had fashioned the road from St Albans to Dunstable into the widest and finest surface on Watling Street. But he had not reckoned with the menace of reckless drivers, for his fine road had encouraged a craze for speed, and Markyate's long and narrow High Street on the route had become the scene of many accidents.

Pickford knew the Markyate hostler would now depend on sympathisers and friends for his very survival, for parish funds set aside for such events had long since been exhausted. So he set two specialists and close associates the task of alleviating the plight of the legless Markyate man.

Markyate folk had cause to wonder when Uriah Spary, one of the finest wheelwrights in the area, purchased three foxhounds. Even more so when he was joined by coachbuilder Charles Walker training the animals to harness. But secret it was no longer when the craftsmen trundled an ornate, minute, specially-designed vehicle on to the High Street and harnessed the dogs to it. It was a dog cart.

It gave Old Lal, who had been housed and maintained by the inn-

keeper in the main stables, a freedom that he had not thought possible. For he found that he could earn money by running errands and delivering packages in the neighourhood.

Everything seemed to favour Pickford's latest enterprise until another unforeseen bogey reared its head. For as well as the highways improving or deteriorating according to the locality, another plight of the passengers, beset by constant jerking and jarring, was the need to endure periods of great boredom. And so it was that the sight of the legless man and his strange chariot caused much comment. It was not long before they were challenging him to race their vehicles through the village High Street. Old Lal found them most generous and began a practice which provoked much local hostility. Even Pickford rued the day he assisted the man. For accidents in the High Street had occurred as a direct result of Old Lal's charioteering. But the old man would not desist, and even changed his humble stable abode for the best room in the Sun as his finances increased. Thomas Pickford was most perplexed, but there was little he could do about it. Then one Sunday morning providence in the form of the local hunt solved the pioneer's dilemma. For just as Old Lal was emerging from the Sun Inn yard the whole village was thrown into an uproar as a fox, hotly pursued by the hunt in full cry, chose the High Street as the best route of escape. Immediately Old Lal's 'motive power' forgot their hours of training and promptly joined in the

69

chase. Furthermore, despite the legless man's protests and strenuous attempts to deter them, Old Lal's dogs got closer to the fox than the hounds of the hunt. And with their quarry within their grasp Old Lal's dogs forsook the highway for the ditches, hedges and fields beyond.

Some hours later a group of subdued huntsmen re-entered the High Street and with great reverence deposited a lifeless body in the Sun yard. They had found Old Lal in a wood where his animals had crashed his cart, wedging it between two fir trees. At the coroner's enquiry held at Hemel Hempstead, a huntsman vociferously claimed it was the fox that had caused the death of Old Lal. But the recorder decided – death from misadventure – and a relieved Thomas Pickford got on with his carrier business.

When Titan clashed with Hercules

On the 10th of May, 1808, there was immense excitement in the counties of Bedfordshire, Buckinghamshire and Hertfordshire.

For days, there had been a vast exodus from London as members of the sporting fraternity, commonly known as the Fancy, deserted their fashionable haunts for the inns of Dunstable and the surrounding villages. The price of a night's lodgings had reached the fabulous price of two guineas, but the supply could not meet the demand for beds.

At first light vehicles of every description began to crowd Watling Street. Farm carts impertinently vied for the right of way with the crested barouches of the nobility, and over the fields, the footpaths and by-ways walked the excited country-folk.

Two days earlier the county newspapers had carried a statement from the magistrates, who warned that they had information concerning a proposed boxing match and anyone taking part in any way would be severely punished.

In Dunstable the officers of the law were much in evidence, but as yet had taken no action. Only a few miles away, however – at Ivinghoe, Buckinghamshire – the fight promoters were facing a crisis. Drawn up in battle array under the county's chief magistrate, the Marquis of Buckingham, the high constables, petty constables and other peace officers of Buckinghamshire were defying the sportsmen to challenge the law. In Bedfordshire, the Dunstable volunteers had been called out under arms and were mustered on the Downs, and upon a given signal the troop moved on Ivinghoe.

In the face of such determined opposition, the fight promoters hurriedly revised their plans and rode off to the estate of Sir John Sebright of Beechwood Park. Thus the fight for the Championship of England came to be staged at Markyate in Hertfordshire.

The fight, which attracted more attention than any contest had done for years, had been made possible by the retirement of Hen Pearce, the famous Game Chicken, the undisputed Champion of England and one of the greatest prize fighters of all time.

There were two claimants to the title, Bob Gregson, a Lancashire giant, and the Bristol-born, former butcher's boy, John Gully. Gregson had defeated all opponents in the north country and had moved to London, where he had opened a tavern which was receiving the

patronage of the Fancy. Gully, who had only been defeated once in his career had already met and beaten Gregson. But it was due to his epic battle with the Game Chicken himself, who was his friend, tutor and benefactor. In that contest it had been felt that the match would be fixed, particularly as the Game Chicken had provided the means of Gully's release from prison. The contest, however, had been altogether genuine, Gully being battered into defeat only after an hour of the most ferocious fighting ever seen. After the bout the Game Chicken retired,

and Gully, having recovered, claimed the right to meet Gregson for the title.

News of the change in plans spread rapidly through the vast crowds, and they turned about and headed along the Watling Street to the village of Markyate. Within an hour Markyate's narrow High Street was crammed with excited people, the inns doing a roaring trade.

At noon some of England's greatest fighters, who had arrived to witness the contest, were greeted with great shouts. All along the High Street men fought with each other for the privilege of rubbing shoulders with the famous Game Chicken, the well known battler Harry Lee, the up and coming Tom Cribb, the fabulous fighting Jew Daniel Mendoza, and many others.

Meanwhile, half a mile away, at Beechwood Park, Sir John Sebright and his friends were preparing for the contest. Sir John had called upon every available man in his service, and these, along with the younger members of the Fancy, armed themselves with cudgels and formed a phalanx ready to intercept any men of the law who might put in an appearance.

A ring, forty feet square, was created, and then encircled as a second line of defence against the law by a barrier of coaches, barouches, wagons and carts. The enclosed area was then divided into sections for the audience. There had been a steady downpour all that morning and the rain showed no sign of ceasing as the crowd thronged into the park and the contestants appeared, ready for the fight.

By the time they were prepared to enter the ring, the press had become alarming. Scores of ruffians converging on the ringside had ousted the gentry from places reserved for them and were creating confusion and annoyance. Faced with this menace, Captain Barclay, who had been appointed as umpire, directed the four ring-masters to use their whips on the ruffians to keep order. The tumult lessened and an air of expectancy descended as the fighters began to strip.

Both men were dressed in splendid silken breeches and stockings and arrayed themselves before the assembly. There came great applause, for the men were considered the finest specimen of manhood in the kingdom. But the betting was in Gregson's favour. Then came disagreement. It was discovered that Gregson was wearing slippers which were spiked while those that Gully wore were not, and it was thought that the spikes would give Gregson a decided advantage on the wet grass.

The matter was settled by Gregson pulling off his slippers and tossing them into the crowd; Gully instantly followed suit. So it was in stockinged feet that the two men finally squared up for the

Championship of England.

For a moment they eyed each other, the rain glistening on their bodies. Then the combatants mixed a fury of blows that saw Gully driven back to his corner. There he was so hard pressed that he was in danger of being impaled on the jagged edge of the corner stake. Immediately his seconds rushed to cover the stake head with their hands, and held this position until Gully escaped and landed such a blow that he toppled the Lancashire giant to the ground.

In the second round Gully revealed further skill. But he first had to sustain a blow from his opponent that made onlookers winch as they heard it land. Gully staggered but dodged the following blow which was thrown with such force and strength that it threw Gregson around. It was Gully's chance. He drove in quickly and a well-aimed punch sent the Lancashire giant down for the second time. Knowledgeable spectators now began to favour Gully rather than Gregson.

Nevertheless, in the next round Gully was badly pounded, finally going down to a mighty blow on the head. And it was Gregson who carried the verdict for the following three rounds, with Gully's face bleeding profusedly and another gash on his right arm, where, in parrying a blow, the force of Gregson's punch broke the skin.

The seventh round witnessed an exchange of titanic blows, and the crowd yelled as the fighters locked in a savage embrace, crashed through the ropes and continued fighting outside the ring. Finally, neither having succeeded in breaking the other's hold, they fell together. Gregson dominated in the eighth round with a fierce two-fisted attack, grasping the battered Gully about the waist and dashing him to the ground. But, although he was now grievously injured, Gully fought the ninth in a lively manner and from then on the science for which he was famed had its effect. For although Gully was knocked down in both the twelfth and fourteenth rounds, it was clear that his carefully placed blows were beginning to reduce the stamina of the Lancashire giant, who was showing signs of distress. For Gregson's left eye was almost closed and his right was constantly blinded by a flow of blood from a cut in his forehead. He charged about the ring swinging wildly, and often blindly. Gully side-stepped these rushes, emiting blow after blow, his opponent being unable to land even once in reply.

The fifteenth round proved to be the most violent of the contest. As Egan Pierce, sports writer of the time, records, 'the blows exchanged were tremendous'. But neither had the strength to follow up his advantage, and both men tottered drunkenly about the ring.

Gregson's head was covered with blood and his left eye completely closed, while Gully's left arm had been rendered useless by parrying a blow which had threatened to dismember him. Yet the fight went on, with the spectators yelling deliriously. Quietening them suddenly, Gregson caught Gully with a blow to the head that sent him down as if pole-axed. Astonishingly, this did not end the fight, for Gully resumed the struggle and, with his good arm working like a piston, he proceeded to batter his opponent's sound eye.

Excitement surged to fever pitch again as Gregson, enraged, threw caution to the winds and waded in furiously. But John Gully retreated cautiously, making the most of the advantage which was now so obviously his. In the following rounds he continued to reduce his opponent's strength with crucially placed blows.

Incredibly, though each had received a terrifying battering, they carried the fight to the twenty-third round. Indeed, it might not have ended then had not Gregson run into a terrific blow which caught him under the ear, leaving him gasping on the ground. Even then the giant tried desperately to regain his feet, but lacked the strength to do so, and, after some moments, the fight was declared at an end.

Amid an ovation which he certainly deserved, John Gully was declared the winner. The contest had lasted fifty-eight minutes and neither man had fallen from exhaustion, and every time one of the contestants had gone down it had been the result of a blow. Gully was barely able to stand as he acknowledged the cheers of the crowd. His left arm hung useless at his side as Sir John Sebright entered the ring to place about his neck the brightly coloured kerchief held only by the man who was the Champion of England.

But to the astonishment of all, Gully refused the honour. He announced that he would fight no more, and therefore would not honour the award, and with that he left the ring with the man he had beaten.

Nor did Bob Gregson step into the ring again; he went back to his tavern, and soon after Gully also took over an inn, the Plough in Carey Street, Lincoln's Inn Fields, London. Surprisingly, in view of the punishment they had taken, both men lived to an advanced age. Gully became a Member of Parliament, while Gregson bought a coal mine. But they gave Markyate that rare distinction of being the place where the two greatest prize-fighters in the land met to decide who was

The Champion of England.

They Came by Night

Between the years 1820 and 1840, a particularly vile type of criminal operated in Britain – the Resurrectionist. The name, familiar if blasphemous, was applied to those unscrupulous persons who made a livelihood by opening graves and selling the corpses to teachers of anatomy.

Though detection meant punishment (and some communities had their own particular method), these men considered themselves as following a legitimate trade, far removed from the stigma of thievery. So flourishing was the trade and so lax the legislative control that it became a temptation to murder. In 1828, an Act was passed to regulate the dissection of bodies, and making it necessary to obtain licences. But in spite of this, grave robbing continued for many years.

The Resurrectionists were particularly active in the Dunstable area. The celebrated nineteenth century Dunstable historian, Worthington George Smith, records an incident affecting his own family. A relative had buried his wife on the Saturday at Kensworth. Early the next morning, before anyone was about, the grief-stricken husband returned to his wife's grave. The body, still in grave clothes, lay in the church-yard beside the grave. In this instance the Resurrectionists had probably been disturbed and went off without the corpse.

But a hole had been dug at the head of the grave, the headside of the coffin broken away, and the corpse drawn out by a hook inserted under the chin. So skilfully was the operation carried out that had the hole been filled in the deed would have passed unsuspected.

The fury which this loathsome practice aroused can well be imagined. At Biggleswade in 1826, a crowd practically tore a grave robber to pieces; it was only by the intervention of the parish constable that he lived to face the justices at Bedford. The record of this case is typical of many which occurred throughout the country.

The deposition of the Reverend Robert George Sucklin-Brown, vicar of Biggleswade, made on December 8th, 1826, states: 'On Wednesday the 6th of December 1826, I buried a corpse in the churchyard of Biggleswade. This morning I caused the grave to be opened, and upon examination of the coffin, it was found that the corpse had been taken away. The linen in which the corpse was buried was in the coffin: the grave from the appearance of the earth about it, seemed to have been recently disturbed.'

Before the justices stood two men, George Lester and William Smith, described as labourers, late of Biggleswade. Both were found guilty of breaking open the grave of John Cooper, and removing his body.

It appeared that Lester and Smith left Biggleswade in the summer of that year and took employment in London, remaining there until the news of a relative's illness brought Lester back to Biggleswade in November. He was joined by Smith on the very day his brother-in-law died. Both men attended the funeral. But that same afternoon, the two went to the home of William Carrington, a carrier and the proprietor of a waggon transporting goods between Biggleswade and London. Carrington told the court that both men were strangers to him; they enquired at what time the waggon left for London as they had two boxes, the property of their master, which they wished to pass on to him. The carrier informed them that the waggon would leave at five o'clock the following morning and the boxes should be taken to his office that evening. However, they said that this was not possible as the boxes would not be ready before half-past four in the morning, but they would bring them to the carrier's yard at that time. So it was agreed, and the two men departed.

Later, Carrington became so suspicious of the arrangement that he spoke to the vicar about the matter and he recognised their description of Lester and Smith. Along with six others, including the parish constable, the vicar hid in carrington's yard. At the appointed time, Lester and Smith, accompanied by another man, arrived carrying a large deal box. As soon as they had entered the yard, Carrington closed and locked the gates. The box was placed by the waggon, and Carrington, walking up, asked what it contained. The men said they did not know, whereupon the carrier demanded that it should be opened. Immediately two of the men made a bolt for the fence and escaped, but George Lester was captured and secured by the constable. A lantern was brought, for it was still dark. By its light Carrington cut the cords which bound the box, and then unscrewed the lid. Inside, partially covered with sawdust, was the corpse of John Cooper.

George Lester was taken to the Catherine Wheel public house in Biggleswade and held in custody. Meanwhile news of the affair had spread throughout the town and groups of infuriated people began to search for Smith and the other man. Smith was discovered in a barn. Despite his protests, he was dragged into the street and severely handled until rescued by the constable. The third miscreant took advantage of the mêlée and made good his escape, but doubtless he avoided Biggleswade for the rest of his life.

Gunpowder Bell

The story of the Gunpowder Plot to blow up the Houses of Parliament has been told more often than any other incident from the records of history, but no one ever relates one mysterious feature concerning it – the ghostly bell which tolled at intervals from the very beginning to the dismal ending of this infamous conspiracy.

The sonorous tones of a great bell first disturbed Sir Robert Catesby, the arch-plotter, as he revealed his initial plan to his associates gathered in his Northamptonshire home.

Catesby stood aghast. The sound seemed to come from within the house, yet there was no bell there. He however ordered a search of his own property. But in vain – no bell of any size could be found. With difficulty he passed the incident off, but according to the confessions made in the subsequent trials, several thought it was an ill-omen.

The plot proceeded. Catesby rented a small dwelling adjoining Parliament House and from its cellars set out to dig a tunnel. He was assisted by Thomas Piercy, Roger Keyes, Thomas Winter and Ambrose Rookwood. Guido Fawkes, a soldier-of-fortune who had been enlisted as a result of his activities in the Netherlands, now joined the excavating party at Westminster and acted as look-out during the day, for the noise set up by the constant hammering, and the vibrations which loosened the nearby earth, increased the danger of discovery.

Catesby and his confederates dug feverishly. Parliament was due to open in the February of 1605, and they had not even reached the foundations of Parliament House. But when they eventually struck the plinth, a wall of flint and stone which was the structure they sought, they met a severe check. It was nine feet thick!

Doggedly they carried on. The tunnel began to cave in; water trickled through from the river, and then came the bell. This time the deep

clangour seemed to come from the very bowels of the earth.

Catesby's house – and now the tunnel. What did the bell signify? The records reveal the alarm of the survivors of that day. Holy water was sprinkled about the floor of the tunnel and the bell appears to have been miraculously silenced, but no one dared proceed with the digging there. The place was abandoned.

Then came news that Parliament had been prorogued until October, and that gave the conspirators renewed hope. Fawkes then discovered a vault directly under Parliament House, which was being vacated by a coal merchant named Bright. As the cellar had direct access to the street, Fawkes, posing as a merchant's agent, secured it. Some days later, barrels of gunpowder, cleverly camouflaged by huge faggots of wood were brought in. Then, with some months to go before the postponed opening of Parliament by the king, the plotters returned to their country homes.

Again the sitting of Parliament was postponed, this time for a month. However, Catesby's informants at Court assured him that King James would definitely open Parliament on the 5th of November. Catesby called another meeting and the final plans were made.

Ambrose Rookwood, a Bedfordshire man, was noted for his fine stud of horses stabled at Turvey. He was to arrange for messengers to relay the news of the death of the king. Catesby was to be informed at a huge gathering of Catholics unconnected with the plot, at Dunchurch in Warwickshire. He would then announce a proclamation establishing the heir-apparent, Prince Charles, or Princess Elizabeth, whichever fell into their hands, as sovereign. The rogues anticipated that the elder son, Prince Henry, would be killed with his father at Westminster.

Meanwhile, one of the conspirators, feeling a twinge of conscience, sent a warning letter to Lord Montagle, a Catholic peer, who took it straight to the king. James recalled the death of Lord Darnley in a similar plot in Scotland and ordered a search to be made of all cellars under Parliament; a nightly procedure which remains in force today.

In the early hours of November 5th, Guido Fawkes, waiting in the cellar, answered a knock on the door. Thinking it was one of the band, he opened it and was surprised and quickly overwhelmed by a party of soldiers. During the desperate struggle in the cellar, Fawkes all but suceeded in igniting the gunpowder; he was dragged into the street, securely bound and taken to Whitehall.

Before the king Fawkes displayed such grimness that the spectators were terror-stricken. He readily declared his intention of annihilating the monarch and his entire court. James was most disturbed. He ordered that gentle methods be used to obtain the names of Fawkes' accomplices, but as these failed fearful tortures followed. But Fawkes would not disclose even one name.

Meanwhile his associates, unaware of his capture, had adjourned to their planned positions. Catesby and another conspirator, John Wright, were at Dunchurch. Four others, Piercy, Rookwood, Christopher Wright and Roger Keyes, remained in various parts of London as part of the plan to secure the heir-apparent.

Then rumours of Fawkes' capture leaked out and sent Piercy and the younger Wright hotfoot to inform Catesby. Upon hearing the news Keyes too hurried off to Dunchurch. Courageously Ambrose Rookwood remained at his post. Then, as it was nearing noon on the 6th of November, with all London in a state of excitement, he turned to flight. Mounted on one of his fastest horses he rode furiously out of London, shouting "Despatches for the King" wherever a crowd barred his path. He gained the opened countryside and raced for the north. On Finchley Common, he overtook Keyes and together they rode on in great fear. Rookwood had a fresh relay of horses housed at the Bell Inn, Colney, but dared not venture into the place in case the news of the plot had preceded them. It was at the Sun Inn at Markyate before they dared take advantage of the animals that were housed in the stables there. Had it not been in such a spurious cause, Rookwood's ride that day – over thirty miles in under two hours on the same horse would have presented an enviable record. The two men resumed their desperate gallop until they caught up with Piercy and Wright at Brickhill, then a little later confronted Catesby with the news.

The troop then turned for Ashby St Ledgers near Daventry, where they refreshed themselves before riding off into the midlands in a vain effort to raise a force sufficient to oppose King James. As soon as the conspirators revealed themselves by taking arms, Guido Fawkes was released from the rack and imprisoned. The king, fearing a rising throughout the country, immediately ordered his men to round up the conspirators – and the hunt was on.

Catesby, who had managed to collect forty men about him, took refuge at Holbeach House in Staffordshire. Here he resolved to stand and fight. As his men fortified the place, Catesby stood drying some damp gunpowder before an open fire in the great hall. Then, once again the ghost began to toll!

This was the third time Catesby had heard the bell. Thoroughly unnerved, he spilt some gunpowder into the fire. The explosion that followed severely scorched him and others standing nearby. Just as the house was thrown into confusion by the incident, a troop of volunteers under Sir Richard Walsh, sheriff of Worcestershire, galloped into the courtyard. It was the end.

Catesby, blackened and blinded, but preferring death in combat to the hangman's noose, led his men into a fierce encounter. He received a mortal wound and staggered back to expire within the house clutching a crucifix to his breast. Piercy and the two Wrights died in the courtyard. Rookwood and Winter, dreadfully burnt and wounded, were finally overwhelmed. Of the original number only seven men survived to make the journey as prisoners to the Tower of London.

Throughout the trials which began in January 1606, the King and Queen sat hidden from public view. No witnesses were called. The written depositions of the prisoners were taken as sufficient proof of their guilt. Sir Edward Digby, Robert and Thomas Winter, Rookwood, Grant, Keyes, Bates and Guido Fawkes each pleaded guilty and died as traitors.

Once more the bell tolled, but this time there was no mystery about it. It was the great church bell of St. Paul's clanging out the occasion of the hanging, drawing and quartering of the last of the Gunpowder Plotters.

The Market-Day Murders

It was nearly midnight when John Stock left the 'Boar's Head'. A cold icy wind chased scudding shadows across a baleful moon and the rough road ahead was rimmed with snow. But farmer Stock was in a happy mood as his horse jogged along. His prize herd had brought rich rewards in the market, and his purse hung pleasantly heavy from his belt. The road home seemed longer and darker than usual, but the gelding knew its way, and as farmer John lolled contentedly in the saddle he felt at peace with the world. They were nearing Coppin's wood where the boughs of leafless trees plunged the highway in deeper gloom. Suddenly his horse gave a snort and halted so abruptly that its rider all but lost his seat. A figure had appeared ahead, cloaked in shadows. Then came a flash and a roar that farmer Stock neither saw or heard as his lifeless body slipped in ungainly fashion to the ground.

News of John Stock's murder created great excitement and alarm. For this was not an isolated case; there had been others, farmers waylaid on their homeward journey from Ware market-place. All had been robbed, and it had been young Simon Stock who had found his father's body on the highway that night. His riderless horse had returned to the farm and set off the alarm. The Boar's Head had become a house of whispers, for all knew that the farmer had spent his last hours there, and deep suspicion arose.

Meanwhile, Benjamin Whittenbury, a neighbouring farmer and close friend of the family, assisted the grieving widow and tried unsuccessfully to get young Simon Stock to run the farm. It was an act of charity on Whittenbury's part when the farms merged, but it was to prove a transaction that saved his life.

Simon was barely eighteen when he represented Whittenbury at both the Hertford and the Ware markets, and eventually entered the Boar's

Head. He had a burning ambition to trace his father's murderer, and, for a young man, went well armed. But he found the tavern an unfriendly place, for no one would talk with him, or sit at his table, but all noted the pistol in his belt. Even so, a newcomer who displayed a tray supported by a strap about his neck, calmly approached the boy, and seemingly ignored the weapon.

"Buy a pie, Master Simon? Fresh this day, they are." Simon Stock smiled as he shook his head but watched the man intently as he moved on.

It was nearing Christmas of 1782 when farmer Whittenbury, flushed by a profitable excursion to Hertford market, made his way to the Boar's Head. It was his favourite tavern and was a lively place in normal times besides being the haunt of many of his friends. He looked around for Simon, for he had seen the boy's horse tethered outside, but the lad was nowhere to be seen. Benjamin Whittenbury drank heavily that night and in good company caroused merrily into the late hours, and it was with a befuddled mind that he headed homeward, unaware another horse with carefully muffled hoofs bore a rider in his wake.

Simon Stock had slackened in his quest to discover his father's murderer, but the more he thought about the Pie Man moving so freely among the patrons at the Boar's Head, the more suspicious he became. The Pie Man, a fellow known as Walter Clibbon, had a small shop in the town, and using some pretext Simon visited the place. He found the place run by Clibbon's wife and his two sons, and decided that he had never seen a more rascally crew. But it was the Pie Man who claimed Simon's close attention, for as a tradesman he could watch and overhear market-day transactions without suspicion. The man would also know whose purse hung heavy and where his victim lived. Simon Stock was very much aware of the Clibbon's movements when his benefactor Benjamin Whittenbury regaled him boisterously in the Boar's Head.

The night air had cleared farmer Whittenbury's head and he sat steadier in the saddle as his mount plodded on. Then as a cloud cleared the wintery moon, the road ahead suddenly shone like a silver thread and outlined three shadowy figures. The farmer dug his heels into the horse's flanks. The mare responded and leapt forward. But something grasped Whittenbury's left leg and he fell headlong on to the roadside. As he rose to his feet the shadows closed with him. He was thrown violently on his back as two figures held him, while a third man rummaged through his clothes.

And this was the scene that concronted Simon Stock as he raced into view of the moonlit villainry. Dragging a long barrelled horse pistol from its saddle sheath he pointed and fired wildly as he rode. Startled, Whittenbury's assailants stood off, and the two who were holding him

ran for cover of the hedgerows. The third man still held his ground and drawing a knife was about to plunge it into the farmer's throat when the hoofs of Simon's great stallion struck him.

The fellow pitched headlong into a ditch, but as Simon turned his horse about he saw that the miscreant had regained his feet and was again assailing the recumbent farmer. Simon clearly saw the cold glint of steel flash in the moonlight as he disregarded his horse pistol and dragged his smaller weapon from his belt.

According to the records of the County Assize, the demented Whittenbury then screamed 'Shoot . . . Stock . . . or I am a dead man.' Simon Stock fired at point blank range, his shot entered the man's shoulder and pierced through to his chest, killing him instantly. But even so his lifeless body slumped on the farmer, the knife cutting deep into his arm.

There was a special sitting at Hertford where it was revealed that no less than five men had fallen victim to the market-day tyrant, and no one had ever suspected the Pie Man. His accomplices had made good their escape and were never traced, but the authorities ordered that Walter Clibbon's body be buried at the scene of his attempted crime. And on the 28th of December 1782 this was carried out. More than two centuries later, and after a succession of wooden posts, the most recent remains suitably inscribed to revive the story of the dastardly Pie Man of Ware.

The Last Highwayman

It was Thursday 11th March 1802 and thousands of Hertfordshire folk had gathered to witness the dubious spectacle of a public execution, and one which proved to be the last of its kind. For years it had been the practice to execute highwaymen at the scene of their crimes, and this was one such event.

But the very size of the crowd that day had caused the authorities great alarm for they had expected some opposition and had taken steps to contain it. But no one had foreseen the gathering of such a multitude. The High Sheriff, who had been charged to conduct the execution, was more perturbed when the coach conveying the condemned man came into sight.

For although Robert Snooks had been convicted of highway robbery, he was a very popular man. His acts of benevolence were widely known and he had many friends. In fact it had been such a deed that had brought about his downfall, and the authorities present had good cause to be uneasy that day.

On a dark and stormy night one year earlier, a postboy named John Stevens had been carrying mail from Tring and Berkhamsted. As was usual the six leather mailbags were to be transferred to a mail coach at Watford.

At a point where the present-day A41 passes under the railway bridge to accompany the Union canal through Boxmoor, John Stevens claimed he was robbed. He told a Hertford court that a man, masked and heavily cloaked, suddenly rode up beside him and thrust a pistol to his face. Before he could attempt any form of resistance, the fellow had grasped the mailbags and made off in the darkness. Stevens had returned to Berkhamsted and duly reported the incident. There was an immediate Hue and Cry and £300 was offered for the man's capture.

Two days later farm labourers found the empty mailbags on the Chesham road, and the search extended into neighbouring Buckinghamshire. By this time it had been established that the bags had contained many valuables, one packet alone contained £500 in notes, while another issued by the Bank of Aylesbury carried an undisclosed sum in ten and fifty pound notes. Many held the view that Stevens was implicated in the theft and that the robber had prior knowledge of the contents, and for a while Stevens found himself under suspicion.

Meanwhile Robert Snooks had taken up lodgings in Southwark, and upon leaving rewarded a young orphan girl who had been set to work in the kitchens of the hostelry by the Poor House authorities; Snooks gave her a bank note which in value was more than she would earn in a year. The gesture caused comment . . . and jealousy, which caused the note to be traced to one of those stolen at Boxmoor. But Snooks had left the area and no-one knew where. Some months later Robert Snooks turned up in Watford where he had the misfortune of witnessing an old woman cast from her cottage by its heartless owner, while another man ruthlessly burned her few possessions before her eyes. It is recorded that Snooks came off his horse in a fury. He severely injured one fellow and threatened to shoot the other. The outcome finally resulted in Snooks buying the cottage and giving the aged outcast money for her needs. He then rode off. But Robert Snooks had used the stolen notes once again and had made further enemies. The two men reported the incident and gave a full description of Robert Snooks. But once again Snooks had departed. This time he made for his native town of Hungerford, and within a few days was recognised and duly arrested. He was transported to Newgate Prison in London and held there until his trial at Hertford.

From all accounts the court had to rely upon circumstantial evidence. Stevens had some difficulty in identifying him as the robber. But a fellow was produced who claimed he had seen Snooks repairing the girth strap of his saddle on the highway that day. The saddle was produced, and it showed signs of repair. But the notes used by Snooks and reputed to be stolen, were not produced. Neither were any found in his possession. However, since he appeared to be a person with no visible means of support, yet had been lavish in recent months, and also was known to carry firearms, it all seemed sufficient proof.

Announcing sentence, the judge declared that the crime was so destructive to the commercial interests of the country that Snooks should not hope for a pardon but be content that punishment should provide a lesson to others. And accordingly he directed John Page, the High Constable, to execute the prisoner at the scene of the crime and to hang his body in chains to rot by the roadside.

But Hemel Hempstead folk complained and were prepared to petition parliament. They were not going to have a body left to rot in their parish. And so the authorities relented. They agreed to bury the corpse at the place where he was hanged.

The final moments were shrouded in pathos. The armed guard that escorted Snooks from Hertford stood by to suppress any opposition, as the man was placed on a cart and the vehicle pushed under the gallows erected for the occasion. Robert Snooks presented a calm figure as he took out his watch and gave it to a woman in the crowd. But at once it was snatched away from her by a fellow who claimed it as his own. He in turn was set upon by others desiring it as a souvenir. Then the hangman began to haggle with the High Sheriff, claiming that he was entitled to Snooks' clothing, this despite the fact that the man had yet to be executed.

The records say that Robert Snooks met his death bravely and was buried on the spot. But a few days later, the dead man's sympathisers exhumed the body and reverently placing it in a coffin they had provided, reinterred the body with two ornate gravestones to mark his resting place. Many years later, their descendants, members of the Boxmoor Trust, renewed them, and there suitably inscribed they remain for all to see to this very day.

Robin Hood and his Hexton Archers

According to the records of the famous Bow Street Runners, in the year 1811, Hexton, on the borders of Bedfordshire and Hertfordshire, was a place to be avoided. Newspapers of the time carried sensational stories of a band of poachers, organised under a mysterious leader who styled himself as 'Robin Hood'. So violent were these men that peaceful folk went in fear of their lives.

Local landowners, being the chief victims of nightly forays, arrayed their gamekeepers in opposition. But the poachers, drilled and disciplined in military fashion and using bows and arrows to deadly effect, caused such casualties among them as to deter even the bravest. In desperation the landowners appealed to the Bow Street Runners for help, and early in December that year, Terence Brady, a brilliant young officer, was hastily despatched to their aid.

At a gathering of all local farmers and landowners he was acquainted with the position. But although it was not known at the time, the very man responsible for the raids was in their midst. For so great was his daring and so carefully kept was his secret that no-one suspected him. Brady was given complete charge of operations, which he commenced by organising small nightly patrols throughout the district. But since his plans were known, he soon ran into trouble. Accompanied by six gamekeepers, Brady himself fell for a cunningly devised ambush in which the enemy, unseen in the darkness, used their weapons with silent devastation. The officer escaped unscathed, but three of his men were grievously injured.

The ensuing weeks saw the quiet wooded hills surrounding Hexton turned into a battlefield, where stealth, cunning and surprise were the factors of success. The Bow Street officer found himself pitted against a leader of exceptional brilliance. Fires were lit, hay ricks, barns and even isolated cottages were similarly attacked in attempts to draw the

93

officer's attention while raids took place elsewhere; and when these methods failed, small groups of poachers were detailed to seek out Brady's force and to engage them in fierce running fights.

After almost a month Brady had achieved very little and had begun to suspect that his plans were known. So courageously he decided to operate alone. Having chosen a very large tree overlooking the village of Hexton, the young officer began a lonely, nightly vigil. On the second night his patience was rewarded, for noting a man leave his house under the cover of darkness, he decided to follow him. The gamble proved successful, for the fellow unwittingly led him to the gang's meeting place, an old mill perched above the neighbouring village of Pegsdon.

From a discreet distance, Brady trailed the band throughout the night, watching their operations and noting the size of their haul and their audacity in using carts to carry it away. Still shadowing his man, the officer waited until with the approach of dawn the gang dispersed, then as the fellow began the return journey to Hexton alone, Brady intercepted him. The fight was fierce and prolonged. For nearly an hour the two men battled in the ditches and hedgerows without either gaining mastery, but with the arrival of two gamekeepers the poacher was soon overcome. Exhausted and thoroughly frightened, he submitted to their questioning and revealed all he knew about the gang and its leader.

Just two miles east of Hexton at Pegsdon, close to the Barton-Hitchin road, stands the 'Live and Let Live', a small wayside inn which reputedly derived its name from the incident which found some fifty men besieged within while sharing out their ill-gotten gains. Brady took the men unawares. With twenty armed and determined men surrounding the place, he called on the inmates to surrender. They refused and, urged on by their leader, prepared to fight to the last.

Reluctant to expose his men to injury, the Bow Street man decided to apply the very method often used by the poacher gang, but this time against them. So he ordered his men to dismantle a nearby hayrick, pile the bundles about the walls of the inn, then in full view of the beleagured poachers, set fire to them. The ruse worked. Convinced that Brady intended to burn them alive, the poachers quickly threw down their arms and, despite their leader's entreaties, ran through the billowing smoke in surrender.

Only the leader, a well known farmer named Henry Grindle, remained resolute and in one last defiant gesture challenged Brady to engage him in mortal combat. But Terence Brady refused. The course of justice, he claimed, was a better champion than he, and Grindle would have to submit to it. However a sharp tussle took place before the man was taken, but with the rest of his gang he was eventually marched

away to answer for the crimes.

Today Henry Grindle is forgotten and only a small wayside inn remains to revive the story of the man who styled himself Robin Hood and led a gang of poachers.

The Feast of
The Damned

Few incidents in history can surpass the pride of Bedford folk whose ancestors caused the destruction of that bastion of tyranny . . . Bedford Castle. For its Lord, Falkes de Breauté, was probably the most powerful despot in England, even the king was wary of him. But concerted action saw him banished from these shores, while the Bedford spirit of resistance to oppression was like a clarion that echoed throughout the nation. But Falkes de Breauté had been warned. For even before his demise Bedford burghers had made their intentions known. They prepared a banquet for their oppressors – and a snare. They called it a feast for the damned.

During the reign of John, the most notorious of Monarchs, Norman partisans, roamed the country at will, pillaging and destroying the homes and crops of a defenceless peasantry. Such a marauder was Vyo de Faldo, a Norman of low birth, born in Buckinghamshire and formerly a member of John's retinue while Richard still ruled. But upon his death de Faldo played an active part in the murder of the designated heir to the throne, Prince Arthur, ensuring his master, John, undisputed claim to the crown.

But once John had secured the throne, many promises to supporters were unfulfilled. So former patrons retired to their halls and castles and waged war on each other, destroying as much as they could in others' domains. It caused the monk-historian, Matthew Paris, to record that "the land was filled with devels".

The Magna Carta gave no respite. King John, in a fury, appealed to the Pope, who declared the Great Charter illegal and promptly excommunicated all those who had enforced it, and sadly all those unfortunate inhabitants of their lands.

De Faldo left Buckinghamshire, as his king was engaged in a struggle

with a former patron ensconced in Rochester Castle. He headed a band of forty highly trained and battle-hardened soldiers and ravished the countryside, looting and slaying as they went. He had blazed a passage of violence and destruction through three counties before arriving, early one morning, upon the sleeping inhabitants of St. Albans.

It was the most fearful visit ever recorded here. De Faldo's men ransacked the place, slaughtering all who opposed them and then turning their attention to the abbey, seeking the wealth within. The abbot opposed them and entreated vainly as a monk was cruelly slain before his eyes.

This act of sacrilege caused a short-lived revolt by the townsfolk who, led by a blacksmith of whom it is recorded accounted for three Normans with his great hammer, succeeded in diverting de Faldo's attention until eventually he was overcome. But then the abbot intervened and offered de Faldo one hundred marks to leave, which he did but not before his men had burned the heroic blacksmith in the market square.

De Faldo's passage through Bedfordshire heralded his arrival before the county town. But here he was hesitant and thought it more prudent to make camp outside. For it was known that Falkes de Breauté was resident in Bedford Castle and he was one despot that even de Faldo chose not to offend. And so it was that Norman glowered upon Norman while the crafty Bedfordians plotted to make the most of it.

Suddenly the streets became alive with people hastening to and from the market place. A great table was erected. A table that strained under the weight of quickly prepared food delicacies. Magnums of rare wine and glittering goblets added to a splendid array. At last the stage was set and those within the castle who were most keenly aware of the hustle and bustle in the market place became very excited. But the Bedfordians had yet to play their ace, and it came in the form of three great platters, each containing a roasted boar's head, the most cherished of Norman delicacies and traditionally reserved for the greatest of occasions. And Falkes de Breauté was most interested when told that the feast was to be held in his honour. But the crafty Bedfordians had seen fit to relate this to de Faldo and advised that he should not delay. So it was, with his men setting up such a clamour as they entered the town and with Falkes de Breauté distinctly alarmed at the thought of being robbed in the heart of his domain, that a battle ensued between Norman and Norman. Meanwhile the artful burghers hastily retrieved all that had provoked the melée, others took great delight in seemingly aiding their lord and master by pitching the dead and wounded of both sides into the river.

De Faldo met a similar fate but de Breauté ordered his body to be hung on the castle walls as a warning to others. However it was a very mystified Norman who returned to his stronghold that day. For the seeds of his own downfall had been sown in the Bedford streets.

The Royal Poacher

Ebenezer and Albert Fox were twins, and they have rightly been described as the most lovable pair of rogues known to Hertfordshire, or anywhere else for that matter. But the local landowners and magistrates found it hard to regard them in such a favourable light. For the Fox brothers virtually made poaching a career, and thereby caused the keepers of the law and the owners of land considerable annoyance, embarrassment and not a few sleepless nights.

Close to the Royal Oak, which comprises the sum total of the hamlet of Chapel Foot, a few miles south of Hitchin, runs a little lane. Now almost abandoned to nature, it has known the stealthy tread of the Fox twins and has often re-echoed to the sound of their guns. Even before they died, Ebenezer and Albert had become legends in the neighbourhood, and they were not only masters of the gun but they were unusually adroit with their tongues.

They appeared before the courts countless times charged with poaching, but always individually, and being very much alike in appearance, they made excellent use of the fact. The accused could always rely on his brother to provide him with an alibi which apparently established his innocence. Two hundred convictions were brought, but in fact the magistrates were so confused, that more often than not, they found it advisable and easier to dismiss the case. Legend has it that on only one occasion did either of the brothers plead guilty and this was Ebenezer, and the plea was made in such unusual circumstances that the magistrates suffered one of their greatest humiliations.

It began because Ebenezer Fox for some reason or other had occasion to call on a friend of his at Biggleswade in Bedfordshire. This friend was an innkeeper who catered for the local gentry and the well-to-do traveller visiting the village. No doubt he found in Ebenezer one who could supply him with game to grace the table for his important customers.

On this particular day the poacher was seated comfortably in the taproom imbibing copious draughts of his friend's best ale, when in walked two distinguished-looking gentlemen.

Ebenezer was never at a loss for words and he was quick to turn everything to his own advantage. The two gentlemen had arrived in an elegant crested coach complete with liveried footmen as Ebenezer had seen, but he was not in the least abashed by such evidence of wealth and station. As soon as he heard them mention shooting and firearms he broke into their conversation and proceeded to exploit his technical knowledge of his trade to interest his listeners.

The shorter of the two men, bearded and with noble countenance and bearing, became so intrigued that he eventually began to question Ebenezer. Ebenezer was in full flow, and to such an extent that he sat down with them at the same table.

It was only then that Ebenezer Fox discovered that he was talking to no less a person than the King of England himself. There is much to be said for Edward VII that he found common interest with one of the humblest of his subjects. But there is more to be said for the effrontery of the Hertfordshire poacher who was not in the least perturbed by the disclosure. For astonishing though it seems, the discussion ended with the shabbily dressed Ebenezer climbing into the royal carriage. He was being driven off to shoot with the highest person in the realm!

It happened that same day that a gamekeeper patrolling the estate of his employer, a Mr Hale, disturbed a poacher. Although the poacher made good his escape the gamekeeper had a good enough sight of him to be sure that it was Ebenezer Fox. The gamekeeper was certain of this as Albert, Ebenezer's brother, was ill and confined to bed. Unluckily for him and even more unluckily for the magistrates, it was in fact Albert. The tale spread abroad that he was ill was but one of the many ruses used to serve as a blind for their nefarious activities and to outwit the law.

The gamekeeper reported that Ebenezer had been poaching and Ebenezer appeared to answer the charge. Long used to the twins' guile, the magistrates were dumbfounded to hear the accused admit that he was engaged in shooting that day, and he further confessed that he was on property where he had not obtained permission to shoot. Having made such astonishing admissions he then denied that he had been on Mr Hale's estate.

For a moment the court was possessed by an electric silence. Never before had anyone heard a Fox admit to poaching. The gentlemen on the bench were completely taken aback but were dubious as to

Ebenezer's claim that he had not been on Mr Hale's property.

"Are you sure of that?" the chairman asked.

"I'm certain, your honour", Ebenezer replied. "And I have a witness to prove it."

"Uh!" snorted the chairman, remembering previous experience. "He'll be one of your kind, too."

"If you mean was he along o' me," the accused said with typical guile, "course 'e was. We went shooting together. In fact 'e took me, your honour."

The magistrates sat bolt upright. Never had they heard anything like this. Here was one of the most artful law breakers ever to appear before a court, a scourge of the countryside and a constant thorn in their side, not only admitting his guilt but prepared to name his accomplice as well.

Ignoring the fact that the case before them concerned the violation of Mr Hale's preserves only, the magistrates in their eagerness to make sure of their quarry at last, blundered headlong into the artfully prepared trap.

"If you were not on Mr Hale's land, where were you?"

Ebenezer furnished the name of a large landowner whose estate was

near Biggleswade. It was an impressive name and the bench felt sure that such a gentleman would never tolerate a scamp like Ebenezer Fox on his preserves.

"What is the name of your accomplice?" asked the chairman.

"Ah," said Ebenezer, making the most of the occasion, "he's better off than me. Like as not you'll let 'im go while I'll do time."

"You will *both* get your desserts," the chairman assured him emphatically. "Who was it?"

"If it please your honour, it was His Majesty the King." In the astounded silence of the court Ebenezer added piously, "God bless 'im."

At that moment a distinguished figure entered the court and whispered to an usher. The usher, looking aghast, hastened to the bench. His arrival there precipitated a spell of whispering, punctuated with incredulous gasps and bewildered shaking of heads.

When at last the chairman looked once more at the prisoner, he did so with a face that was scarlet and his embarrassment was so great that it was only with the greatest difficulty that he managed to utter the three words: "The–case–dismissed."

Dilemma in the Skies

A number of years ago, Hunting Percival's first jet aircraft made its maiden flight over Luton. Few saw it, but those who did will never forget it. For in what was virtually a perfect machine, something went wrong. For a few tense, desperate minutes, years of planning, months of work and the life of the test pilot were in danger. And it was the pilot himself, Dick Weilden, who in the very last minutes, prevented the disaster.

That Sunday morning the hangar doors rolled open and a sleek silver aeroplane was trundled on to the airfield. The slim, gleaming body flashed an extra brightness from the July sun, and the men who had built her were rightly proud of their achievement. The aircraft had been designed to fulfil a unique role, and the manner of its development had been well nigh revolutionary. Great things were expected of the Hunting Percival Jet Provost, for its creators rightly regarded it as one of the finest aircraft ever produced in Britain.

Dick Weilden, an Ace Pilot, certainly had no anxieties about it as he climbed into the cockpit. He taxied across the field, then turned into the wind.

Confident and expectant, the little knot of spectators saw an extra puff of exhaust vapour, and then the Jet Provost was moving like a bullet across the green grass. Free of the ground, she rose swiftly into the blue, cloudless sky. Then the spectators saw their confidence justified. Dick Weilden levelled off and put the 'plane through its paces. The designers, engineers and heads of the firm had seen aeroplanes do remarkable things before, but they had witnessed nothing to compare with the amazing display of aerobatics they saw in the next few minutes.

They had every reason to feel exultant, and one of them grinned his delight at his companions, then set out for the bar of the Flying Club to celebrate. Others followed, and only a mere handful remained when it was realised that something was wrong, and something that foreshadowed disaster.

The 'plane, one of the finest of its kind in the world, had proved itself and was coming in to land, its body a bright flash against the dark green of the countryside. It slipped ever further down, until a fold in the airfield hid it from sight. The few, anticipating a perfect landing as the sound of the engine diminished, turned to follow their colleagues to the bar. A moment later, they whirled, for the machine had roared to full throttle.

To their practised ears this was an alarm, a certain warning that something was wrong. Their anxiety mounting, they saw the 'plane shoot up to circle the airfield like a bird startled from its nest. The group on the tarmac apron increased in number as men came running from the bar, beer glasses in hand, some gesticulating at the Jet.

High above, Dick Weilden knew that they were pointing at his undercarriage. He had been about to touch down when he noticed the fault. His landing gear had locked with one wheel down and the other still in the up position in the port wing. To attempt a landing must mean disaster, for the 'plane would wheel round and keel over on the first impact. The port wing would thrust at the ground, twisting the machine into a whirlpool of buckling, splitting metal, with the test pilot himself at the very heart of it.

The aircraft came in close, the pilot throwing it about in the air in a desperate attempt to release the locked mechanism, but nothing he could do would release it. Nor was there time to take further action, for the fuel gauge warned that the fuel reserves were dangerously low. Whatever action he could take had to be taken at once.

On the ground the watchers now stood silent and despairing. The crash tender dashed on to the scene in response to the call of the siren, but that was all anyone could do, apart from Dick Weilden. And already he had decided on his course of action, a desperate course, for it was the only one open to him. To bale out and abandon the Jet would mean its destruction, and the planning and work of years might well be thrown away. He had made up his mind, no matter what the risk to himself, to save the 'plane.

He knew he could only do so if he got that extended leg and wheel up, which would allow him to make a belly landing. He knew that circumstances and time left him only one hazardous way of getting it up. He must come in low, touch the free wheel to the ground, then swing the aircraft sufficiently as to hit it in a sideways movement.

Dick Weilden looked at the little black dots on the landing apron, then he spun into the wind. He brought the Jet Provost down, inch by

inch, until its lowered wheel was trailing the ground. Then he swung the 'plane very slightly. But it was enough. The hanging leg was knocked up into its starboard wing housing.

So far so good. But there was no time left for another run in. The fuel gauge registered zero. With a skill that no pilot could surpass, Dick Weilden righted the aircraft, and then brought the 'plane into thistledown contact with the ground. The undercarriage made such a light touch that the Jet Provost was brought to a halt without suffering any damage.

Dick Weilden slid back the canopy, climbed out and walked stiff-legged towards the crowd of jubilant watchers. He was relieving his nervous tension with a few well-chosen epithets.

So perfectly had he handled the machine that, within four hours, it was repaired and ready for its second flight. Dick Weilden had snatched success from the very lip of disaster.

The Someries Murder

On the last day of March 1860, a huge crowd assembled before the grim walls of Bedford Goal. Among them were people from neighbouring counties, folk who had risen early that morning to travel many miles for the dubious privilege of watching a murderer hang; for although times were changing and generally people were spurning such spectacles, the doomed man had aroused such widespread indignation by the bestial manner of his crime that his passing was deemed worthy of great celebration. Indeed, it is doubtful if the execution of any other common murderer excited as much attention as did that of Joseph Castle, a young malt-maker of Ware.

Castle appears to have been a misfit in society. He was trained at an early age in what was considered in those days to be a specialist trade. Thus he enjoyed a degree of security in employment denied to most. Yet Joseph Castle constantly abused this privilege, allowing his sour, sullen nature, violent outbursts and irregular habits to cause dismissal after dismissal. At last employers in his native Ware and those in the nearby county town of Hertford would have none of him, and so in the autumn of 1857 he made his way across the county border to Luton, then the largest brewing town for miles around.

At nineteen Castle seemed to have the world at his feet for in Luton he found great demand for his skill. Good fortune also favoured him in his selection of lodgings, which took him to the home of a widow and her three young daughters. The Whitcrofts were generous, sober people. They were staunch supporters of the Church and had earned the friendship of many, and it appeared treated Joseph Castle as if he was one of the family.

The kindness, however, was misplaced. For Castle took advantage of his position by pursuing in a cajoling, wheedling manner the hand of the

eldest daughter, Jane, a likeable girl of 17, and after a whirlwind courtship they were married. But disaster soon followed.

Some disturbance at his place of employment saw Castle lose his job, and a succession of similar occurrences found him in the same unemployed and unwanted position as before. So Joseph Castle decided to return to his home town, and Jane, unaware of her husband's true nature, dutifully accompanied him. Very soon she had cause to regret it, for apart from sharing the home of Castle's parents, her husband, having found employment, took to drinking heavily and abusing her. For a while Jane stuck loyally to her post, even when Joseph savagely beat her, but after one terrible scene the girl decided to leave him and return to Luton.

Jane started out early in the morning, but by noon she had covered only part of the twenty-five mile journey. Footsore and weary, she was glad of rest when a Welwyn family who taking compassion on her plight arranged a lift for her on a coal-cart travelling to Wheathampstead, some twelve miles from Luton. As it was, a very tired and dispirited girl eventually arrived at her mother's house about nine that night. Meanwhile, Joseph Castle, having returned from work, was so furious to discover that his wife had departed that he set out, there and then, to bring her back.

According to the records, Castle walked the whole distance without respite, but it was nearly midnight before he reached Luton. Too tired to go farther, he took lodgings at the Windmill Inn, on the outskirts of the town. The following morning Castle angrily presented himself at the Whitcroft home demanding to see his wife, who was still in bed.

Castle forced his way in and the mother and the two young daughters in the lower room heard him threaten, plead, even wheedle and threaten again until Jane tearfully dressed and finally agreed to return with him, and after an emotional farewell to her family set off with her husband for Ware.

However, once away from the house, Castle's evil disposition asserted itself and several people were attracted by his violent behaviour as the pair walked through the streets. The girl was crying bitterly and Castle appeared to be forcibly propelling her along. His behaviour was even more marked as they neared the open countryside. Even the innkeeper who had housed Castle the previous night noted the pair in passing, and later gave evidence that the husband was raving like a madman. This was also eventually supported by a farmer's wife who was disturbed from her work by the girl's cries. Castle was dragging her along, his face convulsed with fury.

Just south of Luton, close to where the boundaries of Bedfordshire and Hertfordshire converge, there is a formerly well-used path, nowadays forming part of the perimeter of Luton's airport, which leads via the ancient ruins of Someries Castle to Chiltern Green and onwards to Welwyn and eventually Ware. It is a cobblestone way, rarely frequented today, and in parts much overgrown with vegetation. A disused chalk-pit, almost on the county borders marks the intersection of the path with a more recent roughly-made road.

It was at this spot that John Purser, a groom employed at the nearby Someries Farm, discovered a trail of blood as he walked along the path towards Luton. Thinking it had been caused by some wounded animal, he traced the trail to some bushes where he found Jane's terribly mutilated body. So fearful were her wounds that Purser decided there was a madman at large, and returned to the farm, warning two girls on the way to take refuge in the nearest house. Arming himself with a shotgun, Purser returned to the spot with a horse and cart, loaded the body aboard, covered it with sacks and drove hastily into Luton.

At the 'Heron', a public house (now named The Blacksmith's Arms) in Park Street, the body was carried into some stables. The police were called, and very soon a large crowd had assembled as news of the affair spread throughout the town. A posse was quickly formed, and with the aid of six bloodhounds hastily despatched to Luton Hoo, the hunt began. It is believed that this was the first occasion on which bloodhounds were employed on an official manhunt in this country.

A thorough search at the scene of the murder soon revealed the murder weapon, a vicious looking bloodstained knife. The dogs took up the scent and at a rapid pace the posse set off into Hertfordshire.

Joseph Castle was taken at Welwyn and given very short shift. Bound and manacled, he was forced to walk behind a cart to which he was secured while his captors and the bloodhounds followed in the rear. Upon reaching Luton, Castle was taken to the Heron, whereupon, according to the records, he was shown his wife's body, broke down and confessed his crime. So furious was the reaction of the waiting crowd, that Castle barely escaped a lynching, and even after he was imprisoned in the local goal, a small rather insecure place, determined efforts were made to burn the place down, prisoner and all. The small local police force was greatly relieved when reinforcements arrived the following morning and conveyed Castle to Bedford Goal.

Joseph Castle was held in custody from August 9th 1859, the day he committed the crime, until the following March, when he was brought to trial, at which many people gave evidence. The accused appeared indifferent to the proceedings, and in fact was actually seen to be chewing something at the very moment the Judge passed sentence upon him.

Luton people celebrated the execution with a banquet held in the main street. A huge bonfire was lit, and around it people danced and generally celebrated will into the night. Souvenirs, suitably inscribed, were in heavy demand. Some of these exist to this day, as do traces of the cross carved in the side of the chalk-pit to serve as a reminder of the deed enacted there so many years ago.

Silent Passage

Among the human remains disinterred upon the discovery of small Quaker burial ground in Dunstable some years ago were the possible relics of the three men who, with others from Markyate and Redbourn, figured in one of the most amazing incidents in Quaker history.

In the year 1665 when London was in the grip of the Great Plague and prayers were being offered up in every church in the land, six men were arrested because their contribution did not follow the accepted religious pattern.

Rodger Preece, George Brown and William Pudephat were among those arrested for holding an illegal assembly in a barn at Caddington. At the time the 'Dissenter Movement', which included the Society of Friends, hung in the balance. Oppressive measures designed to destroy such bodies saw their members sentenced to long terms of imprisonment and harsh fines which saw families reduced to poverty. Some were sent to penal colonies and never returned to their native land.

In the Spring of 1665 law enforcement officers were very active tracking down and arresting people attending secret religious meetings. Cellars and lofts were searched, and even members of the established church were questioned and urged to advance knowledge of likely offenders. So it was that on a Sunday morning in the April of that year, an informer led a party of lawmen to an isolated shed on the then extensive Caddington Common. They found six men, standing, head bowed in silent prayer. They were arrested and subsequently hauled off to stand trial at Hertford, Caddington being at that time part of Hertfordshire.

Murdock, chief arresting officer gave evidence and described how the men submitted passively but declined to answer his questions. He was however moved to say that he saw no treason in what they did. The men remained silent throughout the trial, refusing even to answer to their names. The sentence was vicious. They were to serve fourteen years in an American penal colony, and after languishing in Hertford goal subsequently conveyed across London to the moorings at Deptford.

According to the log of the Good Star, a small merchant ship plying between London and the New World, the six were the first of a religious sect to be carried as convicts, and several crew members voiced disapproval as the men embarked. But Captain Amos Dobson, as tough a skipper as there was, would have none of it and ordered the men to be taken below and shackled in the accustomed fashion.

That same day the Good Star weighed anchor and slipped down the darkened Thames with the evening tide. An entry shows that an hour later the gloom had become so intense that Dobson ordered additional look-out and despatched a man to the bows. Almost immediately the fellow signalled a warning, and Dobson hurried forward. Together, they watched a great ship loom in the darkness and approach them at great speed. It was of a size and shape that neither had ever seen before, and to add to their consternation the vessel did not seem to be propelled by sails or oars, yet it moved against the tide with great ease. Not a glimmer of light showed aboard the mysterious giant and neither man could even glimpse a movement aboard, but her wash nearly capsized the little Good Star as she passed into the darkness.

The mystery deepened a little later as the Moneur, a French ship which had occupied a neighbouring berth at Deptford caught up with the Good Star, and came alongside. Dobson hailed her skipper. He learned the Moneur had held a mid-stream course down the Thames but had not seen any ship such as Dobson described. Whether or not this incident influenced the Captain's judgement, his ship was in trouble again as they neared Gravesend. The Good Star came to a jarring halt as if she had struck some submerged object, or run aground on a mud bank. Dobson clearly expected to find a gaping hole and torrents of water pouring into the forward hold, for he gave an order to prepare to abandon the ship. But strangely no such disaster revealed itself, and after a terrifying shudder that shook the boat from bow to stern, the little ship righted itself and moved on again. Dobson was thoroughly disturbed and conducted a thorough examination, but no damage whatever was uncovered. So it was a very perplexed captain and a mystified crew that paced the decks as the ship reached the open sea.

In the early hours of the following morning Dobson was aroused by an excited seaman. He hastily donned his clothes and hurried below to the storage hold. Ten casks of water stood side by side as they had been loaded but a few hours before. Now they were empty. And search as he

might Dobson could find no trace of a leak in any. He then confronted the sailor responsible for loading the water, declaring neglect of duty, and despite the testimony of two husky seamen who handled the casks and swore to their weight, ordered twenty lashes to be carried out there and then upon the unfortunate man. But it was apparent that the crew was not convinced and made their views known in no uncertain manner. The log clearly shows Dobson's concern at this stage. Mutiny was sensed when the two men who had been detailed to tend the prisoners demanded to be relieved of that duty. The shackled men, they complained, neither spoke nor changed their position, but stood head bowed as though in prayer. One of the sailors admitted striking one prisoner, drawing blood. But even then the man had maintained his silence. Dobson recognised the nervous tension that gripped his men and was a little more than unnerved himself. He visited the men, and tried to engage them in conversation but failed to do so. Nevertheless, he ordered the shackles to be removed and left even more concerned.

A forced call at Dover for fresh water supplies saw the Good Star's skipper seek out the local magistrate and to account that worthy with all the strange occurences that had befallen his ship. But the official was not impressed and considered he was dealing with a typically superstitious seaman, and severely rebuked Dobson for disturbing him.

The ship's crew were on the point of mutiny when the Good Star left Dover, and Dobson found it necessary to instruct further floggings to maintain order. A day later matters were almost out of hand. A series of strange incidents had culminated in what appeared to be an outbreak of smallpox, the mariner's most dreaded disease. Only those in direct contact with the prisoners seemed to be affected, and the rest of the crew flatly refused to go anywhere near them. To make matters worse the Good Star stood becalmed off Plymouth Sound which, Dobson records, was most unusual. By this time every man on the ship was convinced that the misfortune that had befallen the ship since leaving London was due to the carrying of the prisoners, and each man was certain that even graver perils were in store.

The final mystery of this voyage of mysteries came after the ship had been stationary for ten hours. With their own sails limp and lifeless, the entire crew lined the ship's side as the Royal Navy's latest frigate – The Curlew – swept over the horizon, her sails powered by a strong wind and passed them within hailing distance.

Captain Dobson had had enough. He ordered the lowering of the boats, and without further ado, directed lines to be attached to his ship, and the long arduous haul into Plymouth began. The strange scene attracted other crews whose vessels all seemed to enjoy a strong breeze while the Good Star's canvas remained limp even to the moment the rowers hauled their ship to the harbour walls.

Once at anchor, Dobson took an unusual course and summoned the prisoners before him. He gave Pudephat a letter. This stated that he, Dobson, having been charged to carry the six men to America, had carried out his duty as far as it was humanly possible. He feared that his vessel and crew were victims of strange manifestations, which if continued, might result in the loss of all; he therefore commended his charges into the hands of the local authorities for them to do as they thought fit.

The men were put ashore, but the Plymouth officials would have nothing to do with them, except to hasten their departure from their boundaries. Nor were they hindered in the many parishes through which they traversed on the long trek home. Their arrival was especially welcomed by the 'Friends' and signalled a great and timely revival. As far as the county authorities were concerned, it would seem that they deemed it prudent to overlook the whole affair.

When the Witches Came to Town

The persecution of witches and those deemed possessed of evil powers is remarkably recent. In this matter the law was ignored, and George II who occupied the throne some 200 years ago, did not in fact end witch hunting when he made the practice illegal.

In the middle of the eighteenth century a sort of mass hysteria directed against so-called witches swept through Bedfordshire and Hertfordshire. But the people of Luton can remember with pride that their ancestors did not yield to the spreading madness, but on the contrary set a limit to it.

Two of the victims of this hysteria near Tring were John Osborne and his wife Ruth. In April 1751 the Hemel Hempstead town crier was paid fourpence to announce their impending fate.

People of good character, they were the victims of someone they had justly or unwittingly offended, and who instigated the rumours that they had bewitched cattle at Marsworth which brought about their trial. They were repeatedly dragged through Long Marston pond by a carthorse, an example of one of the three infamous Trials by Ordeal. The wife died; the man survived. The law brought those responsible to justice, but not before the wave of terror had swept into Bedfordshire.

Barely two weeks after the affair in Hertfordshire, two unfortunate women were singled out by some ruthless louts in Leighton Buzzard marketplace as guilty of witchcraft. They so incited the mob against Jane Massey and Catherine Hawkes that attempts were made to seize them at once, the aim being to conduct their examination by means of torture on the spot.

It was fortunate for the two terrified women that there were sufficient sympathisers present to enable them to escape. But this so inflamed their persecutors that they secured enough support to conduct a house to house search to secure them. However, their friends realised that the only way to save the two was to get them away from Leighton Buzzard, and so under the cover of night Jane and Catherine were smuggled into a wagon bound for Luton.

At that time the town had a population of only about a thousand persons. However, the women were taken in by James Wilkins, who, with his wife, lived on the corner of Blackwater Lane, known today as Lea Road and Park Street. Unfortunately the whereabouts of the women became known to their persecutors, with the result that the mob made post haste for Luton. The sleepy little township was violently roused as the lusting crowd passed through Market Hill to assemble on what is now Park Square. Here they were joined by a number of locals, who told them where Jane and Catherine were to be found, and the mob converged on Wilkins' little cottage.

Warned of their approach, James hid his wife and the two refugees in a cellar, where they crouched in terrified silence. The leaders of the mob forced their way into the house and so misused Wilkins that he cried out in pain. His wife, fearing they were killing him, began to shriek with fear, thus giving away the hiding place. All three women were dragged into the street and savagely beaten, and then Jane and Catherine were hurried off to a pond, at that time situated on Park Square.

A horse was called for, as the fanatics were determined to lose no time in showing the Luton inhabitants how Leighton folk dealt with their witches. With a horse to hand, a rope was tied about the waists of the women and the mob stood back to watch.

One Luton man however, decided that the proceedings were illegal and he rode off at top speed down Park Street to tell Squire Francis Hearne at Luton Hoo. On learning what was afoot, he instantly called to horse every available man on the estate and determinedly led the way through the park on into Luton. As the column moved on, others from neighbouring farms joined them until the number amounted to fully fifty men. On reaching Park Street close to the Wilkins' home, the Squire mounted a charge and the horsemen rode at full speed into the assembly on Park Square.

The mob, caught unawares and terried by the sight of the galloping horses, scattered in all directions; some actually sought refuge in the depths of the pond. By this time the townsfolk had gathered in sufficient numbers and gave willing assistance to their mounted fellow townsmen. They not only drove the Leighton witch hunters out of the town, but their Luton adherants as well.

A contemporary of the time said that there were many cracked skulls on Market Hill that day. As for Jane and Catherine, they were saved

from an immersion which would have proved fatal, but only at the very last moment. They were set free and allowed to settle in Luton, and as far as is known they passed the rest of their lives peacefully and inoffensively in the town. Witches, as far as the Luton people were concerned, existed only in the imagination of ignorant folk.

They Saved Luton Airport

"It is respectfully suggested that No.4 Platoon of the No.5 Company, Bedfordshire Home Guard, may officially be complimented on carrying out their duties in such a cheerful and successful manner." That was part of a report made by a local commanding officer in those war-torn years, seemingly so long ago. Yet it refers to the heroic efforts of a handful of men in what must rank as the most dramatic incident in the history of Luton and its people.

Nevertheless, because of the security measures in force at the time, few folk learned of it. But today, as Luton's Airport gains international recognition, those men may recall with pride that it was their gallantry that saved the airport from total destruction.

At the outbreak of World War Two, Luton's airport was very much in its infancy. The airfield less than half its present size, and the sole manufacturing concern, Percival Aircraft Ltd, forerunner of the present Hunting Engineering Ltd of mid-Bedfordshire renown, was limited to one very large hanger and a handful of smaller buildings. The district was decidedly rural, and the airport was linked to the town by narrow, winding lanes.

Although the place then had but trifling military importance, the Germans attacked it on the night of the 24th of September 1940, with two parachute mines. One fell to the north of the factory in open land, causing considerable damage to that side of the factory and to several cottages nearby. The other struck the centre of the factory, crashed through the roof and embedded itself in the storehouse beneath. In that position, and controlled by a delayed action fuse, it menaced the whole area.

This was the situation which confronted John Cunningham, the firm's security officer and leader of No.4 Platoon. He had only six men at his

disposal, and was fully aware of the perilous nature of the position and the need for instant action. The whole place was in danger of imminent destruction, and occupants from the stricken cottages had yet to be rescued.

Having ordered a complete evacuation of the area within the immediate vicinity of the mine, Cunningham was about to deploy his small force to the aid of the people in the damaged houses, when Inspector Sears of the Luton police and a number of his officers arrived. As Air Raid Incident Officer, the inspector requested the platoon's help in rescuing the stricken householders, and in searching and making safe wrecked buildings close to the factory.

It was then realised that the platoon's armoury was situated in the storehouse under the mine, and it was decided to make an effort to get the arms and ammunition out. With the mine expected to explode at any moment the platoon leader and three volunteers burrowed beneath it and removed to safety two machine guns, several rifles and a large quantity of ammunition.

This however did not encompass the daring of these men. For they returned, risking injury from falling debris, and succeeded in removing a number of very precious aircraft.

But the greatest feat of courage was yet to come. By the early hours of the morning of the 25th the evacuation of all people living in the vicinity was complete. The casualties were accounted for and everything now depended on the mine's time fuse.

At 11 o'clock that morning Lt. Armitage a Royal Navy mine expert, arrived after a dramatic dash from Portsmouth, and at the request of the Chief Constable of Luton the platoon leader and his sergeant accompanied the naval officer as guides. Whereon the men entered the factory and stood ready to give assistance while the expert inspected the mine and decided the method of dealing with it.

It lay at an angle to the storehouse roof with its nose partly protruding inside the room some eight feet from the ground. The mine was held in this position by the attached parachute cords which were entangled in the supports of the hanger roof above. While Armitage studied the mine at close quarters, John Cunningham and Sergeant Parrot quickly cleared a path through the surrounding debris in the vicinity of the store to allow for a get-away in the event of a mishap.

Having moved all vehicles, ambulances, fire tenders and a number of cars from the vicinity of the factory, Lt. Armitage and Cunningham collected the necessary tools and began to work on the mine. Perched precariously on the roof of the storehouse, they tackled the first fuse. Knowing that every moment was likely to be their last, they worked slowly and carefully, and eventually succeeded in extracting the fuse. Then they discovered that the fuse they had removed was one which operated if the mine landed in water and thus became 'magnetic'. It was the other fuse that constituted the real danger, and the position of this created an even greate risk.

Due to the angle of the mine and the store roof, the mine's second fuse was almost obscured, and it would be necessary to move the bomb to a vertical position. Courageously the two men exerted every effort to move it. But it was far too heavy, and John Cunningham was forced to call for volunteers.

Without hesitation seven men came forward. They were Sergeants Parrot and Bradbury, Corporal Hills and Private Lillywhite of the Works Home Guard unit, two special constables of the Luton police force, and the works manager. Six of these men entered the store itself, where, using planks of wood, they endeavoured to support the mine from below. The seventh man climbed up beside Cunningham and Armitage and together they began to lever the mine into an upright position.

Then it happened. The parachute cords strained and broke. The mine slipped and a half ton of explosive crashed down amongst the men beneath. For John Cunningham the world lit up in a brilliant flash followed by complete oblivion.

He regained consciousness some minutes later to find Lt. Armitage standing over him. The Lieutenant was smiling and holding in his hand . . . the second fuse. The danger was over. John Cunningham was not the victim of the exploding mine, but of a piece of falling debris which had struck him, knocking him unconscious.

Within an hour the harmless mine was on its way out of Luton. The townsfolk were returning to their homes unaware that John Cunningham was directing operations which resulted in the factory returning to its vital business the very next morning.

For his part in that dramatic incident, John Cunningham was awarded the George Medal.

A Canterbury Tale

There is so much history to be found within the walls of Canterbury Cathedral that it is no surprise to find three small stained glass panels dedicated to a long forgotten Bedfordshire story. For according to the works of Benedict, a monk of Peterborough, that small community of Westoning, almost destroyed in recent years as a result of a petrol spillage, was not a haven of peace even seven hundred years ago. For he records that the villagers were so often drunk, especially during the festival of St. Thomas a'Becket, that they became the laughing stock of the county. But the martyrdom of the archbishop held special significance for Westoning folk. A three day festival was held in his memory and they chose it as the time for hiring labour and for the settling of outstanding accounts. So it was that in the early thirteenth century the taverns of Westoning were echoing with good cheer when a local landowner, much the worse for drink, upset the entire assembly by refusing to pay his dues.

The merrymaking came to an abrupt halt when John Fulke, a hedger and a ploughman, was refused payment for a task that all present knew he had performed. But the landowner was adamant. He, Ailward, would not pay for the land that had been ploughed . . . and that was that. But Fulke, being a popular and genial fellow, attempted a compromise. He would accept half of what was due providing Ailward would keep the merrymaking going by buying beer for the assembly with the rest. However, this made matters even worse for Ailward refused point blank and drew upon himself the abuse and hostility of everyone present; so much so that he left the place in a furious rage.

In his drunken stupor Ailward came upon the ploughman's modest home. Since he blamed the man for the ridicule he had suffered, Ailward decided to teach the man a lesson he would not forget. So

brushing past Fulke's three small children, he entered the house and smashed everything he could put his hands on. Still not satisfied Ailward decided to hinder the ploughman further by taking away and hiding the very tools of the man's trade. And he was in the act of leaving with Fulke's leather gloves and a small whetstone when he was apprehended. For Fulke's children had found their father and warned him, and in company with many others caught the landowner, overpowered him and promptly handed the fellow over to the beadle who represented the local authority. And so it was that Ailward, now in a more sober frame of mind, found himself deposited in the dank depths of the sheriff's goal in Bedford.

He had several days to reflect upon the enormity of his actions before he was hauled in front of a tribunal and closely questioned. But Ailward strongly denied that he had any intention of robbing the ploughman and insisted that his misdeeds that day were due to a befuddled mind. However, his inquisitors were not satisfied and ordered that the man should stand trial at the next assize.

This took place at Leighton Buzzard and is the feature of one medieval plate. Ailward seemingly lost confidence in his ability to prove his innocence and in desperation requested the opportunity to convince everyone by undergoing the infamous Trial by Ordeal.

This was indeed a desperate step. For he knew that his plea depended on survival. But courage failed him as he first declined a trial by combat, knowing the ploughman and anyone that Fulke might choose as a champion to oppose him, would overwhelm and defeat him. So he chose the ordeal by fire. But this time the beadle who had arrested him opposed the issue and the ordeal was refused him. Ailward then knew that the final ordeal, the viscous trial by water, would be forced upon him. Acccordingly the man's right hand was plunged into a bucket of boiling water, the damaged part of the limb quickly bound and sealed and given just three days to recover. The verdict went against him, and accordingly Ailward was condemned to be punished according to the law and the very harsh customs of those times.

It is perhaps surprising that such a barbaric scene should be depicted in such a hallowed place as the Trinity Chapel of Canterbury Cathedral, but Ailward's punishment is the feature of yet another panel. For the unfortunate fellow was taken to a spot near Elstow and, before a large crowd including dignitaries of the church, thrown to the ground where he was held by three burly men and pinned by a great bulk of timber straddling his chest while the executioner carried out his gruesome task. The Peterborough monk does not spare the hideous details. For Ailward's eyes were gouged out, with one left hanging on his cheek; and at the same time he was castrated. He was then left to die on the roadside.

However, Benedict records that there was one among the Bedford burgesses who had compassion on him. For he conveyed him on a cart to his home in Bedford and confining Ailward to a darkened room, nursed the man almost day and night. And after several months Ailward showed signs of recovery. The chronicler says many holy men visited him, claiming that his survival was a miracle to be attributed to the martyr Thomas a'Becket. For Ailward is said to have regained his health, and small bird-like eyes even formed in his mutilated sockets. Eventually, assisted by several pilgrims, he was able to journey to St. Albans Abbey and later to the great Cathedral at Canterbury. Here he was held in great esteem and received rich offerings before his death and subsequent burial within the precincts of the church.

Books Published by
THE BOOK CASTLE

JOURNEYS INTO HERTFORDSHIRE: Anthony Mackay
Forword by The Marquess of Salisbury, Hatfield House
Nearly 200 superbly detailed ink drawings depict the towns, buildings and
landscape of this still predominantly rural county.

JOURNEYS INTO BEDFORDSHIRE: Anthony Mackay
Foreword by The Marquess of Tavistock, Woburn Abbey
A lavish book of over 150 evocative ink drawings.

**NORTH CHILTERNS CAMERA, 1863–1954; FROM THE
THURSTON COLLECTION IN LUTON MUSEUM:**
edited by Stephen Bunker
Rural landscapes, town views, studio pictures and unique royal portraits by
the area's leading early photographer.

THROUGH VISITORS' EYES: A BEDFORDSHIRE ANTHOLOGY:
edited by Simon Houfe
Impressions of the county by famous visitors over the last four centuries,
thematically arranged and illustrated with line drawings.

**FOLK: CHARACTERS and EVENTS in the HISTORY of
BEDFORDSHIRE and NORTHAMPTONSHIRE:** Vivienne Evans
Arranged by village/town, an anthology of stories about the counties' most
intriguing historical figures.

**ECHOES: TALES and LEGENDS of BEDFORDSHIRE and
HERTFORDSHIRE:** Vic Lea
Thirty, compulsively retold historical incidents.

JOHN BUNYAN: HIS LIFE and TIMES: Vivienne Evans
Foreword by the Bishop of Bedford
Bedfordshire's most famous son set in his seventeenth century context.

LOCAL WALKS: NORTH and MID-BEDFORDHSIRE: Vaughan
Basham
Twenty five circular walks, each linked to an interesting topic.

**LOCAL WALKS: SOUTH BEDFORDSHIRE and NORTH
CHILTERNS:** Vaughan Basham
Twenty seven thematic circular walks.

CHILTERN WALKS: BUCKINGHAMSHIRE: Nick Moon
In association with the Chiltern Society, the first of a series of three guides
to the whole Chilterns. Thirty circular walks.

EVA'S STORY : CHESHAM SINCE the TURN of the CENTURY:
Eva Rance
The ever-changing twentieth-century, especially the early years at her
parents' general stores, Tebby's, in the High Street.

WHIPSNADE WILD ANIMAL PARK: 'MY AFRICA': Lucy Pendar
Foreword by Andrew Forbes. Introduction by Gerald Durrell.
Inside story of sixty years of the Park's animals and people – full of
anecdotes, photographs and drawings.

FARM OF MY CHILDHOOD, 1925–1947: Mary Roberts
An almost vanished lifestyle on a remote farm near Flitwick.

A LASTING IMPRESSION: Michael Dundrow
An East End boy's wartime experiences as an evacuee on a Chilterns farm at
Totternhoe.

DUNSTABLE DECADE: THE EIGHTIES – A collection of photographs:
Pat Lovering
A souvenir book of nearly 300 pictures of people and events in the 1980s.

DUNSTABLE IN DETAIL: Nigel Benson
A hundred of the town's buildings and features, plus town-trail map.

OLD DUNSTABLE: Bill Twaddle
A new edition of this collection of early photographs.

**BOURNE AND BRED: A DUNSTABLE BOYHOOD BETWEEN
THE WARS:** Colin Bourne
An elegantly-written, well-illustrated book capturing the spirit of the town
over fifty years ago.

ROYAL HOUGHTON: Pat Lovering
Illustrated history of Houghton Regis from the earliest times to the present.

Specially for Children

**ADVENTURE ON THE KNOLLS: A STORY OF IRON AGE
BRITAIN:** Michael Dundrow
Excitement on Totternhoe Knolls as ten-year-old John finds himself back in
those dangerous times, confronting Julius Caesar and his army.

THE RAVENS: ONE BOY AGAINST THE MIGHT OF ROME: James Dyer
On the Barton hills and in the south-east of England as the men of the great
fort of Ravensburgh (near Hexton) confront the invaders.

Further titles are in preparation.
All the above are available via any bookshop, or from the publisher and bookseller

THE BOOK CASTLE
12 Church Street, Dunstable, Bedfordshire LU5 4RU, Tel (0582) 605670